P9-CRT-419

Backpack to Briefcase

Making a Successful Transition to the Workplace

By Terry Arndt & Kirrin Coleman | A Life After Graduation, LLC Publication | Third Edition

COPYRIGHT INFORMATION

3rd Edition, Copyrighted February 2012

Copyright ©2012. Life After Graduation, LLC. All rights reserved. No part of this book, including cover design and Web site (http://www.LifeAfterGraduation.com), may be reproduced or transmitted in any form, by any means (electronic, photo-copying, recording, or otherwise) without the prior written permission from Life After Graduation, LLC. Printed in the United States of America.

BOOK DISCLAIMER

Life After Graduation, LLC has made its best effort in preparing this book to be accurate and complete. The content of the book is not guaranteed to produce any particular results. In addition, the advice given in the book may not suit every individual's circumstances.

Therefore, Life After Graduation, LLC does not assume responsibility for advice given. As a result, each reader should consider their own circumstances and abilities and weigh them versus the advice given.

Life After Graduation, LLC is not in the business of rendering financial, legal, or any other professional advice. If any questions regarding legal or financial advice should arise, the reader should seek professional assistance.

Life After Graduation, LLC shall not be held liable for any damages arising from the book's content.

ACKNOWLEDGMENTS

Life After Graduation started as an idea for a class project back in 1998. Over the next year, the concept of providing college graduates information that would help them achieve career and financial success as they transition into the "real world" became a reality. Years later, Life After Graduation continues to expand it's number of resources to help college students as they transition into and out of college.

This company would not have become a reality without the support, insight and encouragement of several key individuals, including John Ricchini, Kirrin Coleman, Jeanette Alexander, Jeremy Moff, Jason Williams, Kerwin Burton, Renee Albert, and Carrie Williams.

I also want to thank my family and friends, particularly my lovely wife, Joanna, and our children – Max and Maggie. I sincerely appreciate you supporting my dream – it gets better and better every day!

Terry Arndt

President
Life After Graduation, LLC

DIFFERENT PERSPECTIVES ALL IN ONE PLACE. THE HARTFORD.

At The Hartford, we believe in the power of diversity and inclusion. Our culture engages the many talents, perspectives and potential of our entire workforce. This companywide belief fuels innovation and profitable growth to meet the ever-changing needs of an increasingly diverse marketplace and community. **Learn more at TheHartford.com/careers**

Get the free mobile app at
http://gettag.mobi

2012 WORLD'S MOST
ETHICAL
COMPANIES
WWW.ETHISPHERE.COM

With The Hartford behind you, achieve what's ahead of you.®

THE
HARTFORD

© 2011 The Hartford Financial Services Group, Inc., Hartford, CT 06155. All rights reserved.

SCHOOL OF BUSINESS
CAREER CENTER

Dear School of Business Student:

Let me be the first to congratulate you as you near the completion of your degree from the University Of Connecticut School Of Business. I understand the dedication and commitment that it takes to reach this milestone and I am immensely proud of your accomplishments.

In the *School of Business Career Center* we recognize that as you transition from the world of academics and backpacks into the early stages of your chosen field, you will encounter many challenges. Some of those challenges will be obvious, while others, will be deceptively simple.

This book has been designed to help you navigate the early days of your career. It covers what to expect on the job as well as how to deal with the unexpected. Although students have been introduced to many of these topics in classes, this book will make the important distinction between the way a college student interacts with others and the way a business professional is expected to act on the job from day one!

Is with pleasure that, with the financial support of The Hartford Financial Services Group, the School of Business Career Center is able to provide this book to you. We wish you well in all of your future endeavors. Read on…

Student today, Husky Forever

Sincerely,

Jim Lowe

James R. Lowe, Assistant Dean External Relations / Outreach
Executive Director School of Business Career Center

TABLE OF CONTENTS

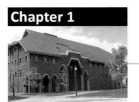

Chapter 1

MAKING A
GREAT FIRST IMPRESSION

Ten seconds. That's about how much time you have to make a lasting first impression. (It's actually a little less time than that, but we'll round it up to simplify things.) Whether you're on a date, at an interview, or on day one of a new job, those first ten seconds have to be good. No biggie, right? Just enroll in some acting classes, hire a vocal coach, work out like a fiend, and convince some cheery talk show host to treat you to a total wardrobe makeover. Oh, and buff the briefcase and shoes. Then sit back because you have it totally made. Right.

Here's the part where your blood pressure skyrockets while we tell you why humans are wired to make snap judgments and how it's really a good thing, a survival tactic we carry with us from the cave to the cubicle. Imagine, after all, the poor caveman who carefully deliberated, weighing the pros and cons of taking action when confronted by a charging bear. There are benefits to the quick appraisal: It saves time and energy. Also, our instincts are pretty reliable. We have inherent expertise that tells us, "Shifty eyes plus muttering plus clenched fists: bad. Nice eyes plus clear voice plus smile: very, very good." We don't have to take a body language seminar to know who's a potential threat and who's a potential mate.

Great, you say. Love the snap judgment when appraising, but it's a little nerve wracking to be the appraised. Plus, all this talk of bears and clenched fists raises the anxiety level a few notches. OK, relax. Because here's the part where we tell you what you can do to ensure you do make a great first impression on your new bosses and coworkers. And it doesn't involve a vocal coach or a total wardrobe makeover.

It does, however, mean debunking some favorite sayings, such as "Looks aren't everything" and "It's what's inside that counts." Yes, yes, but…the truth is that people judge on appearances first, then on personality and performance. So we have to pay attention to how we look and the impression we create.

Grooming and dress

Grooming and dress are the first things people notice about you, long before they know anything about your work ethic or crystalline brilliance. Luckily, it's fairly easy to manage this aspect of your image and it doesn't necessarily have to cost a year's salary.

For any job, you'll want to present a well-groomed, well-shod self. There were exceptions to these basic rules in the mid-1990s, when employees took the looks-aren't-everything maxim to heart and were often spotted coming to work in what might best be termed "pajama casual." In most companies, however, the norm now is definitely a professional or laid-back professional (otherwise known as "business casual") look.

So what should you wear? In some workplaces the dress code is obvious and might even be outlined in the employee handbook. In other companies the rules might be less clear and you'll see people in pinstripe suits working alongside others in jeans and sneakers. Dress according to what you see around you. Pay particular attention to the people who hold similar positions to yours: They are your most reliable resource when you're trying to figure out the wardrobe norms of the organization.

Even in a relatively casual office environment, it's worth dressing up a bit for the first few months of a new job. This is not to say that you need to wear a three-piece suit if everyone around you is in Bermuda shorts and flip-flops. One lesson we all learned in the throes of fourth grade, after all, was that fitting in is important and maybe even be evolutionarily advantageous. However, in the case of your new job, it's better to err a little on the conservative side: A quick study of the best-dressed employee can reveal how to fit in and project professionalism.

Now let's talk about the ever nebulous "casual day." What evil but brilliant clothing marketer came up with this concept? It's ambiguous at best, a cruel and misleading conspiracy at worst. Most of us, after all, have two types of casual: Painting the Town Red and Painting the House. Neither of these constitutes the "casual" in casual day, though if you look around the office you might see some clothes that would fit in well at the nightclub or, on the other hand, paint spattered, torn shorts that are one washing away from the rag pile.

What's Your Company's Image?

Your interview and first visits to the company will probably give you a strong sense of the company's image and how you will fit in with it. The three most common modes of dress in today's workplace are Professional, Business Casual, and Creative. The definitions and descriptions of these categories do vary by company and region, but this chart is a good starting place for understanding your workplace's image.

Dress Mode	Definition	Environment
Professional	Suit or sport jacket with slacks/skirt Collared shirt Conservative accessories Tie (men) Hose (women)	Banking, law, medical, engineering, insurance, sales, management, and accounting
Business Casual	Slacks (cotton OK in some offices) Knee-length (or longer) skirt Collared shirt (including golf-style shirts) Tailored sweater Coordinated accessories Hose and closed-toed shoes (required in some business casual environments)	Technology, education, journalism, retail, government, human services, and science
Creative	Anything goes (within the norms of the company culture)	Marketing, arts, and design

Casual day is ripe for confusion. Usually, it means to dress comfortably without the sloppiness afforded by truly comfortable clothes. So you can wear jeans, but not the holey ones. "Dressy" T-shirts are OK, too. Again, the best guide to what's really appropriate is to consider how higher ups and well-dressed colleagues interpret the dress code. And when meeting with clients, definitely take your look up a few notches.

How to wear it (and how not to wear it)

Here are answers to your most common style questions, as well as a few "don'ts":

How should my suit fit? The jacket sleeves should hit your wrist bone when your arms are relaxed. About ½ inch of shirt should show beyond that.

What's the best blouse fit? A good-fitting blouse will not pucker at the shoulders or chest. If it's a long-sleeved blouse it should hit your wrist bone.

What's the best trouser length? Pants should rest on the top of your shoes in front and go about ½ inch down in the back. This rule applies equally to men and women, though some women's pants are cropped by design.

How many shirt buttons can I leave undone? For men and women, leaving the top one or two buttons undone is generally acceptable.

What color socks should I wear? Match pants, not shoes. Remember that socks should not be visible unless you're sitting down.

What's the best heel height? Shoes with a 1 – 2 ½ inch heel are safe bet. In some organizations, higher heels will be acceptable.

Do I need to wear hose? That depends on the organization. Bare legs and open-toed or peek-a-boo shoes are acceptable in many workplaces.

What's the best tie length? The bottom of your tie should hit the spot between the top and bottom of your belt.

How should I accessorize? Shoes and belt should match each other. Wear minimal jewelry.

What's the best skirt length? Skirts should be knee length or longer.

Your company may have a liberal dress code—or no dress code at all—but there are some hard-and-fast rules to follow if you want to make a positive impression.

Here's a quick list of the major don'ts:

Don't show too much skin. Both sexes: Make sure your V-neck is not too deep. Keep that chest—manly or womanly—under wraps. Also, all clothing should fit well and not be tight or clingy. Women: Avoid spaghetti straps and mini skirts.

Don't come on strong. Douse yourself in perfume or cologne and you could turn people off and/or prompt an allergic reaction. Keep jewelry tasteful.

Don't let your clothes say too much. Clothing with offensive, distasteful, or questionable slogans is best left in the back of the closet. One exception: If you're working for a political campaign, wearing a slogan-covered t-shirt might actually advance your career.

Maintaining a groomed workspace

Unlike the interview, your image now that you actually have the job is a product not just of how well you take care of yourself but also how well you take care of your space. The state of your desk, office, or cubicle (even your handbag and car, in some professions) factors into your overall impression on others.

There's no revelation here, just a reminder to keep things organized and clean, especially in those first few months when you're building others' opinions of and confidence in you. Spend time setting up your office or cubicle and clean out your wallet, handbag, and briefcase.

When it comes to decorating your workspace, keep this in mind: It's an extension of you, a "personalized public space," not a private space. Make it comfortable and personal. It's OK to show off your family and friends, but keep the party photos at home.

Non-verbal communication

Body language accounts for about half of what we say, and therefore comprises a huge part of our image. Try the following exercises to model this point. Stand with your arms crossed in front of you and eyes directed down at the floor. Say, "I'm so happy to meet you" in a cheerful voice. Or, cock your head to one side, raise an eyebrow, smile, and say, "I'll take a look at the data."

You're sending out signals all the time. Your actual words, of course, count for some of what you say. But the tone of voice and body language you employ are much more significant indicators of your meaning. The most frequently cited study on interpersonal communication states that body language and facial expressions when someone is expressing feelings and attitudes account for 55% of meaning, tone and quality of voice account for 38%, and the actual meaning of the words count for just 7%.

Eye contact, posture, fidgeting…all of these non-verbal cues can reinforce or sabotage what you verbalize. Be aware of what your body is saying. You might even want to spend some time in front of a mirror, evaluating your "neutral position" (the way you carry yourself most of the time, when you're not actively engaged in conversation).

Here are some attributes of "positive" and "negative" body language:

"Positive" Body Language
(Signals interest, confidence, enthusiasm, and/or approachability)

- Nods head

- Uses hand gestures for emphasis (excessive gestures may signal aggression, however)
- Has erect posture
- Smiles
- Blinks at a regular rate
- Body takes up space (stance, posture, and arm position say, "I belong here")
- Cocks head slightly (shows interest, but can be interpreted as confusion or flirtation)

"Negative" Body Language
(Signals boredom, insecurity, annoyance, and/or aloofness)

- Pins arms to side or across chest
- Handshake is limp or overpoweringly strong
- Slumps or hunches over
- Frowns, grimaces, or clenches jaw
- Expressionless, blank face
- Blinks too fast or stares
- Body closed off (stance, posture, and arm position say, "I don't want to take up any space")
- Fidgets excessively
- Rolls eyes
- Yawns or sighs

While it's easy to adopt a professional wardrobe even if you've been living in workout wear for the last few years, it's challenging to make over your body language. After all, you've had decades to adopt the unconscious quirks that make up your body language vocabulary. Also, your posture, expressions, and gestures are more indelibly you than a shirt or shoes, and can't—and shouldn't—be discarded willy-nilly.

A few adjustments, however, might help you in your professional life. If you tend to sit back with your arms crossed during meetings, you'll project disinterest and maybe even resistance to new ideas. Reminding yourself to sit upright and to lean forward a little when listening to others could project a radically different, and more successful, image. Just being more aware of your image will help you change it.

Verbal communication

Of course, while nonverbal communication accounts for an enormous part of one's image, verbal communication is still important. The average person says thousands (sometimes even tens of thousands) of words a day. So what, exactly, are we saying?

The truth is that some people don't know what they're saying or how they're saying it. Yet, communication skills are not optional, a bonus accessory some professionals happen to have; they are vital for every professional. Your success on the job is inextricably linked to the way you communicate.

What's your communication style? Do you say what you mean? Do you say it effectively? What do you inadvertently communicate to others when you talk to them? Take stock of your verbal communication skills and polish them if necessary—you'll be glad you did.

Communication styles can be influenced by a variety of factors, such as culture, gender, personality, and education. Everyone has his or her own personal style. Of course, that style is also dependent on one's surroundings: You probably won't use the same tone and vocabulary around your supervisor as you do your good friends. Understanding your own style as well as the different types you might encounter in others will give you an advantage in communicating with a broad range of people and will help you communicate more clearly. Here are some elements to consider:

Rate of speaking. Do you speak rapid-fire or back-porch? If you speak too fast, you risk losing people and/or appearing insecure. If you speak too slowly, you risk boring people and/or appearing, well, slow. Confident people know that others will listen to them, so they don't rush through their sentences. Considerate people know that they are not the only ones with something important to say.

Volume and clarity. You have good ideas and the skills to put them into action, but no one will know this about you if you mumble or speak too softly. Speak clearly, enunciate, and project confidence.

If you're really serious about assessing your verbal communication style, the best thing to do is to watch a video of yourself interacting with others. Be objective as you view the "evidence." Try to notice, not judge, your "ums," "ahs," "likes," and other inadvertent conversation habits. Consider these questions: How much time do you give to other speakers? Do you interrupt frequently, sometimes, or not at all? Is your voice audible? How do you physically present yourself? Many people find watching themselves on video about as pleasant as appendicitis during rush hour traffic. However, if you can get past the initial discomfort you'll find it's an invaluable exercise.

Another helpful practice is asking a trusted friend or family member to give you some honest and constructive feedback. Or find a group like Toastmasters International (www.toastmasters.org) that will provide an opportunity to practice public speaking in a non-threatening environment. It's a big—and for some, scary—commitment, but when you think of it as an investment it becomes clear that a little time and self-reflection now will pay off big in the future.

Email and Instant Messaging

Another way to make a positive (or otherwise) impression is through email and other electronic means. Here are some key points to remember about electronic communication:

Tone: Email and IM are so pervasive, it's easy to forget how artful some of the messages need to be. Word choice, punctuation, and capitalization (plus an emoticon or two, maybe) are the only clues your reader has to your tone. Before you write an email, think about how you can communicate this information best. Sometimes a phone call or face-to -face conversation is better. If you think an email message is the best method for the situation, do take the time to compose your messages. Also, pause before you send. And with emotional emails of any sort, pause for at least 24 hours.

Face-to-Face vs. Electronic Communication: A decade ago, it would have been unheard of for next-door employees to email each other. But now it's such a creeping norm that some companies have taken the radical step of announcing no email days in order to engage employees in more face-to-face interaction. Go with the norms of your organization, but remember that in-person communication is a great way to build real relationships.

Privacy: Ha. Privacy is SO early 20th century. Email only those things you'd feel comfortable posting on the staff room fridge. If your father likes to forward every off-color joke and visual that's ever circulated the Web, tell him in no uncertain terms that he needs to remove you from his contact list. Or he'll be supporting you for the rest of his life. IM is not as easy to track and monitor, but work is work, and it's best to save the personal material for home. In fact, many organizations have strict rules against using company technology for personal matters. Another thing to note: If you have a MySpace or Facebook account or blog, remember that it might be viewed by someone from your workplace.

Relationships with colleagues

OK, so you're well dressed, perfectly postured and enunciating with the precision of a broadcaster on network news. Your desk looks like the cover photo of a lifestyle magazine. Now what? Well, now you've got to play well with others.

You have a budding relationship with your boss already, which will develop according to the natural dynamics of boss-underling relationships. But equally important are the relationships you build with other people in the company, whether it's your boss's boss, the human resource coordinator, or the receptionist. Once you've been hired the real scrutiny begins, because your new coworkers have their chance to size you up. As the newbie in the office, you will fill several functions in addition to the official duties of your new job: stranger, rookie and, sometimes, source of entertainment. Anxious yet?

No problem. Yes, the first 10 seconds are critical, but you have months and even years to build relationships with these people. And while the focus of this chapter so far has been on outward appearances, a good working environment depends on real people bringing out the best in each other.

These tips will take you beyond the introductions and into the early months of your new job:

Show interest. Be open to and interested in all the people you meet at your new job. Really listen to them, whether they're instructing you on the fine art of not jamming the copy machine or telling you about their volleyball league. Ask questions, make eye contact, try to remember specific details. People appreciate and respond to those who are sincere, engaging, and curious. Conversely, the quickest way to turn others off is to appear self-centered and aloof.

Be generous, but not too generous. Give compliments, offer to buy a round of coffee, bring in treats for the staff room. But don't do any of these things too early or too much or you may come across as insincere or desperate. Acceptable for these early days: "Cute kid!" or "Nice spreadsheet!" Unacceptable: "You have great eyes!" or "You're the best boss ever!"

Project a positive attitude. Make sure that your net contribution to the office atmosphere is positive. Positive, energetic, professional, eager to work—all of these are traits of successful people. You might not always feel full of pep, but it's important to act like you're happy at your job and ready for business. In fact, you'll often find that acting energetic will improve your mood and actually give you the energy you need.

Respect your coworkers' time and expertise. You will probably need a lot of help figuring out office procedures and protocols. Asking for guidance from coworkers is one way to get to know them. Quick requests for recommendations—the best deli, the nearest dry cleaners, a good gym—can be great conversation starters. If you need something that will take more than a few minutes of a coworker's time, however, ask if you can set up an appointment. That way he or she will know that you value his or her expertise and time.

Accept invitations. In these early days on the job, you want to accept as many invitations as possible. It might be tempting to do a solo lunch so you can study your employee manual, but the most important thing to do at this stage is to connect with the people you work with. One cautionary note, however: If the conversation during these outings with colleagues heads towards gossip, be aware of your position as the new kid on the block and maintain neutrality. The trick is to be sociable without getting sucked into a clique.

Connect with all players. Everyone in the organization is important. While support staff (receptionists, secretaries, administrative assistants, office managers, and IT support) might have smaller paychecks than CEOs, they are generally very powerful people in the company. Why? They have the keys (literally) to the supply closet, have access to top management, and can get you assistance when you need it fast. When you're on deadline and the copy machine goes down, you want the go-to person to be there for you. If you've cultivated a good relationship with him or her, you'll be in good shape. Also, support staff knows everything about everything: They can tell you which days the boss is in a good mood and can even help you minimize a mistake if you've made one.

Winning over coworkers isn't about faking them out, but about putting your best self forward. It will help you professionally and personally if you showcase your best attributes in these early days on the job. As American author Kurt Vonnegut once said, "We are what we pretend to be, so we must be careful about what we pretend to be." If you want to be poised, articulate, personable, engaged and engaging, organized, and positive, act like you already are that way. This attitude and way of being will serve you well beyond those early, first impressions and soon you'll see it's not just about how others see you, but about how you see yourself.

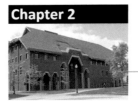

Chapter 2

UNDERSTANDING YOUR ORGANIZATION

The robots of this world can judge how good a work situation is with hard, quantitative data: Add salary (X) to benefits (Y) and advancement potential (Z), then divide by commute time (C). That's it. The job is good if it pays well, offers a fancy title, and doesn't take two hours and three trains to reach. But experienced professionals will tell you that the feel of the company is critical to job satisfaction. Yep, the feel. Or, in office speak, the company culture.

Each company has a unique personality, composed of its values, structures, and behaviors. When you first get the job and begin to develop the skills and procedures that relate to your position, you'll also start to figure out the organization's culture. More importantly, you'll begin to understand how you interact with this culture.

It's kind of like moving to a new country: Some of the traditions and expressions will seem familiar immediately, while others become clear with time and translation. Because job satisfaction directly relates to how well the organization's personality meshes with your own, you'll want to get the lay of the land early on. Consider this chapter your guide to understanding your organization. We'll provide a thorough definition of organizational culture, map out how you can assess your organization's personality, and offer tips on how to work with it.

Two ears, one mouth

There's an old saying that we have two ears and one mouth because we're meant to listen twice as much as we speak. Keep that saying in mind as you navigate the first weeks and months of your new job. Interviews are meant for showcasing your achievements, impressing everyone with your knowledge, and just plain selling yourself. But after the interview is over it's time to show how well you adapt, which means more watching and listening and less talking.

Here's how to start out right:

Watch. Observe body language and how people in the company interact. Where do people gather? Who are the leaders? How much space do employees give each other? Is it a heads-down environment—everyone working quietly in their cubicles or offices—or more open and collaborative? Do people take breaks? What are the workday norms—is it a 9 to 5 office that really shuts down at 5:00 p.m. or do people tend to come early, work late, and take work home?

Listen. Listen to the way people communicate with each other. Do they share ideas freely? Is it an outspoken environment or more reserved? Casual or formal? How do colleagues talk about their work? How do they talk about customers, clients, coworkers, and management?

Ask questions. Learning about the company and your new job can feel like you're drinking from a firehose, but try and absorb as much as possible without getting overwhelmed. Ask questions that will help you understand the company better as well as your role in it. Carry a pad of paper and pencil with you so you can take good notes of everything you learn. Remember that no one expects you to know everything right off the bat so they'll see your questions as a sign of interest and a willingness to learn and adapt. It's better to ask early, too, because at some point you will be expected to "just know." Another way to gather valuable information is by reading—read the employee manual, company literature, the website, and all emails that come through your inbox.

Implement what you learn. Once you get the lay of the land you'll be confident you know what's expected of you. Then it's simply a matter of doing it. Look to the leaders of the company as models of job performance. You'll find leaders—engaged, enthusiastic, and productive people—in every department and at every level, from management to support staff. By observing the ways of others, you'll soon get a sense of how to operate successfully within the organization's environment.

Company culture

As we mentioned in the introduction, company culture is a product of a combination of values, structures, and behaviors. You'll pick up on some aspects of your new workplace's culture as early as the first interview. The environment itself reveals a lot about the company's values: From the layout of the office to the casual interactions between colleagues you'll find clues to deciphering the unwritten "codes" of culture. Here are some ideas to help guide your assessment:

Mission and vision. Is there a clear, shared company mission? Do your coworkers speak positively about the company and its leadership? Does every employee feel invested in the future of the organization? Successful, dynamic businesses depend on a shared vision.

Expectations and support. Are standards and expectations clearly defined and attainable? Do supervisors encourage and nurture employees' success on the job by giving timely and constructive feedback on their work? Are mentors available? Is there a clear evaluation/annual review system? These qualities not only foster your ongoing professional success but also ensure that you're respected and that your contributions are valued.

Physical office structure. Does the office layout say hierarchy or anarchy (or, more likely, something in-between)? An open floor plan with shared workspaces hints at a collaborative, non-hierarchical organization, while rows of cubicles surrounded by closed-door offices suggest a highly stratified environment.

Work habits and hours. What are the standard hours employees keep? What are the productivity expectations? Do your coworkers have working lunches and "breaks"? Are employees expected to volunteer for additional projects? Get a sense of what everybody's doing early on so you can adjust your pace accordingly.

Communication. What are the most common modes of communication used within the office? Face to face? Email? Phone? Little sticky notes? What do you see in meetings? Does one person control the agenda? When there is tension, do the people involved treat each other respectfully? Less important are the number of disagreements around the office as the way they are resolved.

State of the staff room. Is the staff room a hub of interaction or basically unused? If the lunchroom is a gathering place, take advantage of the time to meet and get to know more people. Oftentimes these informal conversations are inspiring and will help you recharge. Of course, some staff rooms breed whining or, worse, gossiping. If this is the case, respectfully avoid it as much as you can.

Flexibility. Does the company allow or even encourage flexible work hours? Can employees job share or reduce their full time status if they want to? Remember, these options may not seem relevant to you now, but circumstances change. The more a company recognizes that you have a life outside of work, the better.

Resources. Resources might include technology, postage, food, and office supplies. How liberal is the company with its stuff? How does one go about procuring a toner cartridge? What kind of documentation is necessary? Whatever your company's "available resource" profile, be sensitive to norms regarding office supplies.

Turnover. Do people tend to stick around or does the organization have a more fluid workforce? Of the longstanding employees, who are leaders in the organization?

There may be other elements involved in your particular organization's personality, but these are the most common to consider. Once you have a clear reading you'll see how you can work within the culture.

Working within your organization's culture

Your office's culture will have a profound effect on your life at work and outside of it. Expect that the organization is going to influence you at least as much as you influence it, if not more.

As with other parts of your life, some of the most important rules are the unspoken ones. Follow the ones that add to a positive environment. For example, your company may value the holiday party, and for that reason alone, you should, too. So, if you're trying to decide whether to attend the holiday party or not, think about the impression you'll make if you do attend (or the impression you'll make if you don't show up.) It's tough to give up a Saturday evening in December, but it's worthwhile and will likely mean a lot to those you work with.

The Importance of Participation

GOOD TO KNOW

Some rules simply aren't outlined in the employee handbook— for instance, whether to contribute to so-and-so's baby shower gift, if you should join the softball team or not, and when to go out for lunch with the group. Participate when:

- The activity or event involves team building.
- Doing so will demonstrate appreciation (the holiday party, for example, takes a lot of planning and effort).
- It will allow you to sustain and establish relationships in a way you wouldn't otherwise do in the office.

Some norms are better broken or ignored. Even the most positive workplaces might contain a group that thrives on gossip, undermining, or other detrimental behaviors. Of course you'll want to avoid spreading gossip or getting too close with anyone known for spreading gossip. If you detect a clique, be friendly with the members in a way that is respectful but keeps you a safe distance from becoming part of the group. That way you won't end up inadvertently alienating yourself from colleagues outside the clique. Other bad habits to avoid include complaining, bad-mouthing, and lax expense accounting on business trips. If the norms at your organization are too far afield of your best judgment, you might want to consider switching jobs.

While there are guidelines and tools to help you assess your organization's personality, there's no simple, objective formula to predict how soon you'll feel like "one of the natives." If you're lucky, you've landed in an organization that feels like a good match, a place where you can learn and grow comfortably.

However, even an imperfect match can be instructive. When you learn to work well within a challenging culture, you hone skills that are incredibly helpful in the long run. Keep your overall personal and professional goals in mind. You'll be able to learn from all experiences and apply the knowledge you've gained to a long and rewarding career.

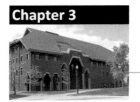

Chapter 3

REALISTIC EXPECTATIONS

You've heard of sticker shock and culture shock, but here's a new condition you should know about: Reality shock. Reality shock is the state many recent graduates find themselves in a week or so into their first job, when their expectations for the job collide head-on with the reality of the organization's expectations of them. So if your eyes ache from the flash of the copier machine and the blur of entering data, know this: Everyone starts somewhere.

Open up a copy of Forbes or Fortune and scan the pages. All those high-powered executives? You can bet that almost every one of them put in their time filing, copying, entering data, and doing all the tasks considered, well, boring. The vast majority of professionals paid their dues in the early years of their career.

However, articles and stories that celebrate successful people often gloss over the boring stuff and head straight for the critical plays, breakthroughs, and stellar accomplishments. We want to hear about someone collating and three-hole punching about as much as we want to hear Uncle Dave's "when I was a kid I walked three miles each way to school" stories. And when most of what we know about the working world is based on television or magazine profiles or even textbooks, it's not surprising that most of us suffer from at least a little reality shock.

We hope this chapter will help you set realistic expectations for yourself, understand the most common causes of reality shock, and see what you're doing now as one step in a successful career.

The importance of having realistic expectations

Did you ever get so excited for a gathering or a big trip that when the actual event came it was anticlimactic? Not that it was bad, but it just wasn't what you imagined somehow. That gap between anticipated excitement and reality can be a let down. And even if you are generally an optimistic and motivated person, it's not uncommon to get so excited by the job search and hiring process that when you start the daily work it seems, well, just like work. Contributing to this feeling is the great sense of accomplishment you get when you graduate: Here I am, World! Qualified! Degreed! Skilled! Energetic! Master of my field! And then someone asks you to change the toner.

If you feel this reality shock you are by no means alone. In fact, the most common complaint of new hires after two weeks on the job is that it isn't what they expected. The good news is it's no longer a complaint after two months on the job. The message here is clear: Give it time. In the meantime, learn about the most frequent causes of new job dissatisfaction.

Employer needs/new employee needs

It's natural to start a new job ready to hit the ground running and prove yourself. You are smart and motivated and eager to become an integral part of the team. Your employer probably hired you for all of these reasons and will ultimately be happy to let you work to your fullest potential. However, it's possible that your needs and your employer's needs in these early days are not the same. It's not necessarily that they are at odds with each other, but more that they're operating at different speeds. You want to run with your talents and take an active role in the organization; your supervisor needs to train you and evaluate your skills and level of commitment. The organization is investing time, energy, and money in you and needs to see evidence that you're invested, too.

You can expect, then, that the early days will involve training and sometimes repetitive tasks. Employers generally like to ease new employees into the scene and provide them with background information as well as a chance to get used to the office norms. Some organizations' training programs are very comprehensive, designed to teach every aspect of the organization to every employee.

Know the history:

Good To Know

"Know how long your position has been around and how many people have held it."

~ **Mary K., California**

Your position in the organization might be newly created or it could have a history. If it's a new position, you'll want to know so you can help define expectations. If it's been around, you'll want to know about your predecessor's successes and failures so you can learn from them.

Whatever the reason for your new-hire job duties, remember they hired you because they're really busy and need help. Right now you might be stapling and changing the occasional ink cartridge, but once they see you care about the job you'll be on your way to doing other things that are more in line with your goals.

Here are some things to keep in mind on these early days on the job:

Everyone starts somewhere. Even the head of the organization has spent time copying, collating, and entering data.

Demonstrate initiative. Volunteer for projects and tasks. Your main goal at this point, after all, is to get to know the ins and outs of your new organization.

Be positive. Your positive outlook and willingness to contribute will be noticed.

Do a good job. This one might be intuitive, but it bears repeating. Whatever your assigned task, do it carefully and do it well. Every action should convey your attention to details and ability to produce quality work.

Be patient with yourself. It can be frustrating to learn the ropes at a new job. It's typical to make mistakes in these early days. On top of that, you may feel slow and inefficient. Don't worry. You will get the hang of it. Focus on one task at a time.

If you need to ask about the tasks you've been assigned, try to begin the question with an "I understand" statement. For example, say "I understand the value of this training process, but I'm curious about when I can expect to transition to other tasks." This will show your supervisor that you're ready to move on without making it seem like you're resistant to instruction.

So far we've assumed you might be dealing with the reality shock that comes from not being given what you think is meaningful, challenging work. There are other types of shock, though. Sometimes you'll land in an organization that is so slammed with work that you get all sorts of interesting, high-stakes projects—and no training. A situation like this can make even the most competent person feel completely overwhelmed.

To make the most of it, ask questions of available coworkers, and try to learn by example. It's a challenge to face such a steep learning curve, but it can be incredibly rewarding in the end. In this case, your employer's need—to get someone who will learn and produce fast—might be a great jump start to your career with the organization. And chances are you'll end up feeling like an integral player in the organization's success.

New Employee Needs	Organization Needs (supervisor and coworkers)
Challenging tasks	To know that the new employee is competent
Autonomy	Evidence that new employee is trustworthy and understands his/her function in the organization
To feel valued	Proven commitment and loyalty
To feel he/she belongs and is liked	Evidence new employee is making an effort to fit in and respects others' time and space

Other common causes of reality shock

In addition to the gap between the organization's needs and your own, there may be some other unexpected realities of work. Following are some of the most common surprises:

Bosses. Your direct supervisor and other bosses will have a big impact on your experience in the organization. See Chapter 8 for more details about types of bosses you might encounter.

Salary. Many people just entering the workforce overestimate their initial salary potential as well as the frequency and rate of promotions. Raises, too, are on average much lower than television or corporate lore would have us believe. Your workplace's human resources department is a good place to start asking about standard promotion and salary practices for that organization. You can also look online for regional norms if you want to get an outside perspective.

Workspace. Another sometimes jarring reality is the workspace you'll have when you first start. A cubicle, a corner of the staff room, a shared table. If you're disappointed with your placement, just keep in mind that your status is a function of how you see yourself, not where you sit or the age and model of the computer you've been assigned.

Work hours. Other common surprises include time demands. You might be hired for what seems like a forty-hour a week job, but end up putting in many more hours learning the ropes and doing what it takes to complete the tasks you've been given. You will get more efficient as time goes on, but it's also possible that the organization survives on lots of people working lots of hours. Or even just a few people working lots and lots of hours. If that's the case, you'll either get acclimated to the time spent on the job or decide to shift gears.

Fitting in. If one of the other feelings you experience is a lack of a sense of belonging, rest assured that this is typical at first. Your new coworkers are busy and won't necessarily go out of their way to meet the new person. But take heart. With time you'll get to know each other and the relationships will develop naturally. Do what you can to connect with them: Ask them questions about their interests, invite them to join you for lunch, and accept invitations they extend to you.

Whatever your experiences in the first weeks and months of your new job, try to keep your ultimate goals in mind. At some point in the not-so-distant future, you'll be doing the work you want to be doing.

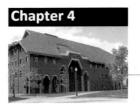

Chapter 4

PROFESSIONAL COMMUNICATION

In business either you're a good communicator or the company will have to hire someone to do it for you. As a strong communicator, you're more marketable and more competitive. You have a better chance of getting the job and at excelling in your profession.

Lucky for you, you have lots of chances to practice your communication skills. Every email you send, voice mail you leave, memo you write, and video conference you attend is another opportunity to make a connection with colleagues, supervisors, and clients. Of course, there's also the risk of miscommunicating. The stories of accidental "Reply Alls," wrong recipients, and inadvertently offensive emails could fill a book. It's important to understand that communication is quick, but what you say, what you write—and how you communicate it—will have a lasting impression. In short, while you can always make amends for a bad communication, you'll be better off if you get it right the first time.

This chapter covers the most common forms of professional communication and how to use them to your advantage.

Telephone communication

The phone is an essential tool of modern business life. Make your telephone communications as professional and effective as possible by following these tips and suggestions:

Answer calls with a professional and friendly greeting. Your greeting should include your company's name and your name. For example, "Good morning, this is Joe Smith at Organization Such and Such, may I help you?"

Smile during calls. Smiling actually affects the way you speak and will make you seem friendlier, even over the phone lines.

Ask the caller his/her name. Doing so—and using his or her name throughout the conversation—indicates that you are interested in him or her.

Speak clearly and slowly.

Avoid chewing gum or eating while on the phone.

Avoid multitasking (typing or reading, for instance) while on the phone. Your caller will be able to hear the distraction in your voice and/or hear the sound of you keyboarding.

Speak at an appropriate volume. If you normally speak loudly, lower your voice. Those who speak softly should raise their voice so the caller can hear them easily.

Speak clearly. Keep the phone about the width of two fingers from your mouth so as not to muffle your speech.

Be considerate about putting someone on hold. Ask the caller if it is okay to put him or her on hold, then thank him or her for holding once you return.

Transfer carefully and politely. Transfer callers to the appropriate person if necessary, instead of transferring them to the operator or telling them to call another extension. Let the caller know that you are transferring them, to whom you are transferring them, and why.

Take effective messages. Messages should include the caller's name and company, time and date of call, subject of call, if and when the caller wants a return phone call, and a phone number at which the caller can be reached.

End calls with a pleasantry, such as "Have a nice day," or "Thank you for calling."

Leaving voice mail messages

In your work life, you may find that you leave more messages than you have real-time telephone conversations. When leaving a voice mail message:

Be brief and get to the point immediately.

Be pleasant and polite.

Speak in a clear, concise manner. You want to ensure the listener is able to hear your message.

Include the basics. At the very minimum, the date and time of your call, your name, a return phone number, and the subject or reason for the call. Spell your name out if necessary.

Give your listener some context. For example, "This is Janna Wong. We met at the trade show last week in Phoenix and discussed potential new business products."

Provide a reason to call you back. For example, "Please call me back so we can continue our great discussion and possibly move forward with the new product."

If necessary, explain the consequences of not calling back. For example, "This is Beckett Jones from accounting. I need you to call me by 5 p.m. today to discuss the bill of your client, Mr. Smith. If I don't speak with you today, I won't be able to bill Mr. Smith until the next billing cycle, which will put your account in the past due category."

Finish your message by repeating your name and telephone number.

Recording voice mail greetings

Your voice mail is often the first point of contact a client has with you, so make sure that you create a clear and professional recording. Here are some tips for making a good voice mail greeting:

Be brief.

Establish your identity immediately. For example, "Hello, you have reached the desk of Patricia Murray."

Sound friendly, positive, and confident. Smile while you record your message and take the time to enunciate.

Tell the caller what to do. For example, "Please state your name, your phone number and the reason for your call."

Give other options, if possible. Some callers want to hear a human voice. If you can, tell callers that if they need help immediately to dial a certain extension to transfer them to the operator, an administrative assistant, or a coworker who is familiar with your clients and work. Or, give them another way or reaching you, such as your cell phone number. This method also cuts down on the number of messages you will receive, so you won't have to wade through multiple messages every time you step away from your desk.

Indicate in your message when you will be available. For example, if you are away on business or vacation, let the caller know in your message that you are out of the office and when you will be returning.

Personal calls

It's common to mesh work and home life. Most of us take work calls at home, check our work emails, and finish up projects after official office hours. Similarly, many of us make personal calls from work or send emails to friends and family members. However, it's important not to let the two worlds get too intertwined or to spend too much time at work on personal matters. Many companies have clear guidelines regarding engaging in personal matters at work. And, while many employers understand that the occasional call home is necessary and won't interfere with the employee's overall performance, other employers have very strict rules forbidding such personal use of company resources.

If you must make a personal call or send a personal email, do so on your own cell phone during your lunch hour or other breaks. Keep personal calls on business phones to a minimum, and only for emergencies or for very short calls with completely benign subject matter. Never discuss sensitive matters on business phones and don't make personal long-distance phone calls from work.

In most states, calls made from a place of business can be recorded and monitored, although most of the time you must be made aware that calls are being recorded. Your employer will also most likely have access to records of phone calls made and received at your phone extension. While phone use is generally not strictly monitored, if a supervisor begins to notice that your personal phone use is excessive, you might be subject to more scrutiny. And, in certain businesses, like customer service or government contracting with security clearance issues, phone calls may be more closely monitored.

Instant messaging

When you need to communicate RIGHT NOW, IM is one of your best tools, but it does have its pitfalls if not used correctly. Here are some helpful tips:

Some like IM, some don't. Know which category your recipient falls into *before* you IM him or her.

Use it sparingly. Otherwise, you might get ignored in the future.

Keep your IMs to one conversation. Multiple IM conversations on your desktop may look like a chat room to your supervisor.

Ask "Do you have a sec?" before you engage someone via IM. No one likes to be interrupted without their consent.

Emailing

It's so easy to dash off an email. Type up your message, hit send, and—voila!—it's out there. Because we use email so frequently and so often for informal communication, it's important to remember its purpose and role in the professional world. Here are some tips for emailing in the workplace:

In general, use the standards of good business writing (see the *Written Communication* section on page 35).

Write with a purpose. Do you need the recipient to take action or provide you information? Do you need to provide information? People get a lot of clutter in their inboxes, so make sure you send only vital messages.

Be brief and get to the point.

Be direct yet cordial. Don't ask the recipient to read through a long chain of correspondence to get up to speed. Provide him or her with proper context and a directive.

CC with care. When cc-ing someone, let the main recipient know that you're including someone else in the correspondence and let the person who's being cc'd know why he or she is included.

Give emails useful subject lines. Tell your readers what the email's about. Avoid empty subject lines like "Hi" or "FYI."

Don't mix content. Don't put a reminder about the fun lunch on Friday in with an important request for a client proposal. The important information might get lost. If you need to address two different subjects, send two different emails.

Don't feel pressured to reply. If someone sends you an email that needs no further action from you, don't respond with a "Thanks" or "Got it."

Write every email as if your boss is reading it. You never know who your email will be forwarded to. Or if your boss is actually reading your emails.

Don't send emotional emails. Discuss emotional or difficult issues face to face whenever possible.

Recognize that (email) tone is in the eye of the beholder. A 2006 study published in the Journal of Personality and Social Psychology revealed that people correctly interpret others' tone in email communications only about 50% of the time. However, we consistently overestimate our ability to communicate and interpret tone. The cute, joking email might sound sarcastic; the clear, direct email might sound aggressive. Don't take it for granted that people will "hear" your words the way you intended them to sound.

Use plain text. Keep everything about your message simple and clear.

Avoid using cute abbreviations or symbols.

Avoid all caps and exclamation points. CAPS ARE THE EQUIVALENT OF SHOUTING! So is the exclamation point!!!!!

Beware the "Reply All" button. When replying, you have two choices: Reply and Reply All. The reply response will generate a message to the person who wrote the original email. Reply All will send your reply message to every recipient of the original email. So, for example, if a coworker sends out a message to 40 colleagues informing them of a meeting, and you hit Reply All in response, all 40 of those people will get your "I'll be there," response, which is not necessary. Only use Reply All when it's appropriate.

Include a signature. Every email you send at work should include your name, title, your company name, your work phone number and your work e-mail address. Some companies even have standards for employee email "signatures," and ask you to include a logo, a link to the company Web site, or other information.

Respond to your email messages promptly, but don't check your inbox continually throughout the day unless you have to. It's too distracting. Instead, set aside specific times during the day to read and respond to emails, such as first thing in the morning, after lunch and again before the end of the day.

Beware of unfamiliar email address. Never open attachments from strange email addresses. Sometimes viruses can even generate emails from real email addresses in your email address book. If an attachment looks strange or is unexpected, even from a known sender, call the sender to find out if it is legitimate.

Personal use of the Internet at work

Check a score, read the headlines, play a game of solitaire, comparison shop, purchase a gift, book an airline ticket, trade stocks…all in a day's work. Or, rather, all in a day's personal use of the Internet at work.

Most employees admit to engaging in nonproductive Internet activities once in a while. According to Nielsen/NetRatings, 92 percent of online stock trading occurs from the workplace during work hours and 46 percent of online holiday shopping takes place at work. And, while most companies accept that employees will spend a limited amount of time on the Internet for personal reasons – checking their bank account balance or their personal email account, for example – corporate America also realizes that personal Internet use can be a problem.

That's why more and more companies are shoring up their Internet use policies and spending both time and money to monitor the ways in which employees use the Internet. Companies are watching. And they don't necessarily do it just to be nosy. Employees that engage in illegal activity via the Internet also put their company at risk for legal action – or at the very least, public embarrassment. Plus, productivity can be significantly impacted by lax Internet use policies. Companies have every right to protect themselves by ensuring that employee Internet use is appropriate. Avoid potential conflicts by following these suggestions:

Know your company's Internet use policies. Does your company frown on any use of the Internet at work? Or do they allow a limited amount of personal Internet use? Perhaps you can use the Internet for personal use, but only during your lunch hour. Does your company use a monitoring system? And what is the policy on handling inappropriate content that might be forwarded to you by a coworker? Know the rules and follow them.

Limit or avoid personal Internet use. It can become a habit—one that negatively impacts your performance at work. It can also negatively impact your employment status: According to the American Management Association, nearly one third of U.S. bosses have fired an employee for inappropriate Internet use.

Use the Internet for personal use as if your supervisor were looking over your shoulder. If you would be embarrassed if your supervisor saw the content you are viewing, you've crossed the line. Incidentally, many companies do monitor their employees' Internet use.

Write every email from work as if your supervisor or other superior at work might read it. Email messages written at work are actually owned by your company – meaning that, if they want to, just about anybody in a position of authority can read them. Because off-color content can expose an organization to lawsuits, many managers feel they have a responsibility to monitor employee emails.

Secure your computer with passcodes and other measures so that others can't use your computer terminal without your permission. You may trust your coworkers, but what about vendors who are wandering through the office, service providers who visit to make repairs after hours, or new employees you don't yet know? Make sure you are the only one who uses your computer.

Keep it clean. Let friends know that it's not okay to forward off-color jokes, pornographic video clips, or other inappropriate – or just plain annoying – content to you via email.

Even if your company does allow a limited amount of personal Internet use and you take advantage of it, some things are off-limits no matter what. These include:

Job searching. Searching for your next job on company time is in bad form and could get you fired.

Pornography or other inappropriate content.

Gambling or other gaming. Using the Internet to do fairly important personal tasks like checking your bank account balance or emailing a child's teacher is often considered OK, but playing games is a clear waste of time.

Illegal downloads. Downloading pirated software or other content is illegal and can put both you and your company at risk.

Personal downloads. Downloading a song to listen to while at work might be OK; downloading entire movies or album collections that might jam up the server and slow everyone down is not.

Instant messaging. Many workplaces allow or encourage employees to use IM, or instant messaging, to communicate with each other, but it's a good idea to check the policy before you download instant messaging software on to your work computer. Keep your IM-ing appropriate for the workplace, as it can be monitored and retrieved. As with any potential distraction, it's good to know when and how to disable IM so you can focus on your work.

Working remotely

According to the Telework Research Network, between 20 to 30 million people in the U.S. work from home once a week and another 15 to 20 million people are so-called mobile workers or "road warriors." Those numbers do not include the millions of people who work from home full time.

Here are some communication tips for the off site or online professional:

Be social. Even though you're not on site, you can have a professional and social presence in the organization. Many remote workers find they can tap into the "water cooler" conversations by staying connected through IM or the organization's chat boards or intranet.

Be seen and be available. Connect with coworkers and supervisors on a regular basis. Provide status updates to your boss so he or she knows you're on track. Make sure you can respond to a phone call or email as quickly as you would if you were in the office. If you can't reply to an email in depth right away, acknowledge that you received it and let the sender know you'll get back to him or her.

Choose the best medium for your message. This advice is appropriate for any work situation, but when you work off site it's especially easy to rely on email, IM, and other forms of text communication. Sometimes, though, a real-time phone conversation or a video chat is the most effective and efficient means to communicate.

Don't rely on one channel. If you can't get a hold of somebody via email, give them a call.

Know how to video and audio conference. Many organizations depend on video and audio conferencing, especially for their remote employees. Here's how to conference well:

- Test equipment and your connection in advance so that if you run into problems you'll have time to troubleshoot.

- For video conferences, make sure there's no glare from a window or bright light.

- Wear solid colors for video conferences. Light pastels and muted colors are best. Avoid very dark, white, or busy-patterned clothing.

- Turn your cell phone off before the conference so you won't be interrupted.

- Avoid making big gestures or quick movements during video conferences and avoid making noise (coughing, eating, tapping fingers, and rustling papers) for both video and audio conferences.

- There may be a delay, so be careful not to talk over other participants.

- Mute the phone when you're not speaking so others won't hear the background noise of your environment.

- As with in-person meetings, avoid checking your email or Blackberry. Refrain from participating in side conversations.

Written communication

It's essential to know how to present yourself and your ideas in writing. We've already covered some tips specific to emailing and instant messaging; the following are strategies for professional written communication in general:

Know your intended audience. Ask yourself, Who is my audience? Who will read this? What is this reader's background, attitude toward me, and attitude toward my subject matter? What does my reader know about my topic?

Be aware of an unintended audience. Ask yourself, Who else might end up reading what I write? Could anything be misconstrued by unknown readers?

Identify your purpose. Ask yourself, What is the purpose of my message? What action do I want my reader to take after reading my document? What do I want my reader to know or understand? What attitude do I want my reader to have?

Select your format. Does your subject call for a formal business letter? An email? A memo? A report?

Choose your ideas. Before you write your document, decide what needs to be included in it.

Organize your ideas. Arrange your ideas in an appropriate, meaningful order.

Choose your tone. Can you be casual and throw in a funny line or two for coworkers? Or should the tone be more formal because it's for a potential client?

Stay focused and on topic. Don't bury your ideas or requests in a lot of fluff.

Be clear. Don't put too many ideas into one sentence.

Avoid wordiness. The business and academic worlds sometimes breed jargon. Why say "Customer utilization of the product achieved peak performance through increased efficiency and accessibility" when you mean, "Customers used the product more when they had more access to it."

Avoid redundancy.

Read your letter/email/memo aloud to catch ambiguities and errors.

Revise and rewrite. If necessary, ask a coworker to read your work and give you feedback.

Edit. Check spelling, usage, sentence structure, and punctuation. You could have incredible ideas, but if your document has errors in it people might think you're not a credible source.

The basic business letter. You should understand the parts of a business letter and how to write one well. However, note that your organization might have its own format or template.

Business letters should include:

- Date (including month, day and year).

- Sender's address. Including your address is optional. Do not include it if the letter is on letterhead.

- Recipient's address. Use U.S. Post Office format for addresses.

- Salutation. Use the name on the address to greet the reader. If you know the person and address him/her by first name, it's fine to use his/her first name (Dear John:). In all other cases, use the personal title and full name followed by a colon (Dr. Mary Doe:). Leave one blank line after the salutation.

- Body. The first paragraph should include a friendly opening and the main point of the letter. Subsequent paragraphs should justify the main point and include supporting information and details. The last paragraph should restate the purpose of the letter and, if necessary, request some type of action.

- Closing. Capitalize the first word only ("Thank you" or "Sincerely") and leave four lines between the closing and the sender's signature.

- Enclosures. Indicate any documents enclosed with the letter.

- Typist's initials. These indicate who typed the letter. If the sender is the typist, omit these initials.

There are various styles of business letters. The two most common styles are the block and indented formats. Examples of these have been provided on the following pages.

Block Format Letter

Life After Graduation, LLC
PO Box 11205
Bainbridge Island, WA 98110

June 19, 2012

Ms. Recent Graduate
Chief Executive Officer, Apex Company
12345 1st Street
Anywhere, USA 56789-1479

Dear Ms. Graduate:

This is the first paragraph of this letter. It should state the purpose of the letter or the reason for writing. This may be the only paragraph that gets read. Therefore, be brief and clear. Write and rewrite until you get it right.

This is the second paragraph of this letter. Most business letters will have more than one paragraph. In addition, the standard business letter will also include some essential elements including the heading, date, address of recipient, salutation, body of text, complimentary closing, handwritten signature, and the name of the sender typed below the signature.

There are, of course, variations of the standard business letter. Be sure to ask your supervisor what, if any, variations you may be required to include in the business letters you write.

I am closing this letter so that I can demonstrate the final elements of a business letter.

Thank you for reading this letter and for reading *Backpack To Briefcase*.

Sincerely,

(signature here)

Terry Arndt
President

jma

Indented Format Letter

Life After Graduation, LLC
PO Box 11205
Bainbridge Island, WA 98110

June 19, 2012

Ms. Recent Graduate
Chief Executive Officer, Apex Company
12345 1st Street
Anywhere, USA 56789-1479

Dear Ms. Graduate:

This is the first paragraph of this letter. It should state the purpose of the letter or the reason for writing. This may be the only paragraph that gets read. Therefore, be brief and clear. Write and rewrite until you get it right.

This is the second paragraph of this letter. Most business letters will have more than one paragraph. In addition, the standard business letter will also include some essential elements including the heading, date, address of recipient, salutation, body of text, complimentary closing, handwritten signature, and the name of the sender typed below the signature.

There are, of course, variations of the standard business letter. Be sure to ask your supervisor what, if any, variations you may be required to include in the business letters you write.

I am closing this letter so that I can demonstrate the final elements of a business letter.

Thank you for reading this letter and for reading *Backpack To Briefcase*.

Sincerely,

(signature here)

Terry Arndt
President

jma

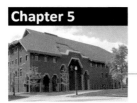

Chapter 5

ETIQUETTE IN THE WORKPLACE

Being courteous, caring and thoughtful to your colleagues isn't just polite – it's good for your career. And while our parents might have taught most of us the basics (don't talk with your mouth full, say please and thank you, don't leave the front door open), workplace etiquette can be a little more complex. The problem is that some of the rules are unspoken, so sometimes we don't even realize we've messed up until we a colleague shoots us a look or we find a sticky note on our lunch bags. Not to worry, however. This chapter will give you the low down on workplace etiquette.

Using office resources

Working in an office means using shared resources, including copiers, telephone systems, printers, and the office supply closet. Every office has different protocols regarding these resources—some, for example, have entire IT departments to handle maintenance and repairs on all computer systems and accessories, while others call repair services only as needed—and you should familiarize yourself with these protocols as soon as possible. During your first week at your new job, ask someone to demonstrate how to use all office machines and the best ways to access resources. Also, find out to whom you should report low supplies, repair or maintenance needs, and problems. Some other things to keep in mind:

Leave it like you found it. Leave paper trays full, work areas neat, supplies on the right shelf, and fax machines cleared of all numbers.

Take initiative to address problems as they come up. If you notice the "Low Toner" light is blinking while using the copier, don't ignore it. Replace it or alert the person who can replace it. It may take a few extra minutes and a little bit of hassle, but you'll be happy you did it when someone does the same for you.

Don't hoard resources. Few things are more frustrating than trying to locate the paper cutter, stapler, or other supplies only to find out a colleague has stashed them in his/her workspace.

If you break it, own up to it. If you jam the copier, short out the fax machine, or topple a stack of office supplies in the closet, admit it, then try to remedy the situation. If it's beyond your capabilities – the copy repair service needs to be called, for example – let the proper person know about the problem so it can be addressed immediately.

Use the fair warning system. If you know you are about to receive a 40-page fax, or need to print a 200-page document on the shared printer, let everyone know so they can plan around it. If you're making hundreds of copies but a colleague needs to make only one, take a break from your job to let her/him cut in.

Common spaces

It's a common occurrence in office life: the note tacked to the break room bulletin board or stuck to the communal fridge by a well-meaning office manager, receptionist, or other employee delegated the job of cleaning up after those who don't clean up after themselves. *"Please clean up your mess!"* Just a friendly reminder, usually after a six-month-old mold-infested container has been unearthed in the fridge, or coffee grinds have littered the sink for the tenth time that week, or dishes have been left, unwashed, in the sink for days. It seems like common sense to clean up after yourself at the office, but when days are busy and distractions are many, it can be easy to let some things slide— especially when someone else will probably pick up the slack. Here's how to do your part:

During your first week of work, find out the rules of the common spaces. For example, is coffee there for everyone, or only for those who pitch into a monthly "coffee club"? Who makes the coffee—the first one in the door, or the office receptionist? Are the dishes and mugs in the cabinets for everybody's use or do you need to bring your own? Do you empty your own wastebasket into a larger trashcan or dumpster, or does a custodian take care of it? Does the office recycle paper, cans, and newspapers? Figuring out office policies early on will help you avoid making a faux pas.

If you mess it up, clean it up. This office golden rule includes all communal spaces like kitchens, break rooms, bathrooms, meeting rooms, reception areas, as well as parking lots and outdoor eating areas.

Wash your dishes and clean up your messes immediately. You may think that you'll do it later, but you may forget during the busy day. Also, while your messes are waiting for "later," your coworkers are noticing the mess and trying to figure out who left it.

If you use the last of something, replace it. This includes toilet paper, coffee filters, paper towels, etc. If the stock room is out of a supply or running low, let the proper person know so he/she can reorder.

Cover your food with a plate or paper towel when using the microwave. It's easier to avoid splatters and spills than to clean them up. And, there's nothing worse than going to use the microwave and finding that it's covered with baked-on spaghetti sauce!

Leave no trace. If you bring a lunch in the morning, remember to bring whatever is left at the end of the day home with you. Don't leave it in the fridge for "later."

Make sure your food is tightly covered. Others might not appreciate the smell of it.

Dispose of garbage, trash, and recycling in the appropriate receptacle.
Most organizations have a trash service that only empties trash every other day
or, possibly, only once a week. Don't use your office wastebasket or communal
trash cans to dispose of potentially smelly or unusually messy waste. Instead,
empty soda cans completely before recycling them, take food items that spoil
straight to the dumpster, and dispose of your used tissues in the bathroom
when you have a cold.

Be mindful of the custodian. The person who cleans the bathroom, vacuums,
polishes the furniture, and washes the windows, has a difficult enough job
already. If you make an out-of-the-ordinary mess on the floor while shredding
documents, spill an entire container of soap on the bathroom floor, or leave sticky
marks on the conference table, do your best to clean it up, or, at the very least,
apologize and let the proper person know what has happened so it won't be an
unpleasant surprise.

Pay attention to the general cleanliness and tidiness of the office, especially
if it is considered everybody's job to keep the workplace in order. If filing is
piling up, furniture needs to be dusted, or clutter needs to be controlled, take
the initiative to pitch in. People notice when you do nice things—and will be
inclined to join you.

Living the cubicle life

The corner office with a view is practically part of the American Dream. But,
most likely, your first office will be housed in that staple of modern office life:
the cubicle.

Many offices use a system of dividers to section off work areas, or "cubicles."
Other offices have an open floor plan with desks arranged into "pods." You
will probably be sharing an office with one or more people and might even be
relegated to a corner in a communal area like the copy room until a better office
space can be found. Working like this can sometimes feel like living in a goldfish
bowl, and the irritations of sharing space are quickly apparent. Make cubicle life
easier—for everyone—by keeping in mind a few tried and true rules:

Noise travels. When working in close quarters, noise is part of the deal. But don't
contribute more than your share. While in the office keep your cell phone on
vibrate or turn it off. Use the speakerphone only when absolutely necessary. If you
are allowed to play music while working, keep it at a volume that only you can
hear. Keep in mind that your voice projects. And forego the convenience of email
alerts for the sanity of your coworkers.

Smells aren't all good. Not everyone loves the smell of broccoli casserole, corn
nuts, perfume, or potpourri. Enjoy foods with strong odors at home. That goes
for scented candles, potpourri, air fresheners, and strong perfumes and colognes
as well. What might be a pleasant aroma to you could trigger an allergic reaction
for a coworker.

Keep personal things personal. Always remember that the partition of your cubicle or the thin walls of your shared office offer limited privacy. Assume that everyone can hear everything and act accordingly.

Respect others' privacy. Sometimes we have to give others the illusion of privacy so that we can enjoy the same illusion. Working in small spaces means that occasionally you'll probably hear or see more than you want to. You might overhear a coworker arguing with his or her spouse on the phone or dealing with creditors; if that happens, just pretend you didn't notice. If they want to share it with you they will.

Keep it neat. Working in cubicles or other shared spaces means you need to do you part to keep your workspace reasonably clean, organized and clutter-free.

Program your office and cell phones to ring at an appropriate noise level. In addition, program your voice mail to pick up after just a couple of rings.

Use meeting rooms for meetings. Brainstorming for a project is best done behind closed doors, where it won't bother anybody else. It may be easier to squeeze everyone into your cubicle than reserving space and time in a meeting room, but your coworkers will appreciate it if you make the effort to preserve their quiet.

Knock before entering. It may seem silly to knock on a cubicle when there's no door, but it's good manners to ask someone if it's a good time before you interrupt.

Taking a break

Sometimes you just need a break. Review your office policies regarding breaks. Do you get a paid lunch break? Is it one hour or one half hour? Are you allowed additional breaks throughout the day? Some offices don't formally outline their break policies, but instead rely on their employees to use good judgment. If this is the case with your employer, ask a fellow employee how breaks are generally handled, and observe others' behavior to figure out what is acceptable.

The lunch break

A lunch break is a given at nearly all businesses. However, every workplace has different rules and protocols regarding lunch breaks.

Some office buildings have cafeterias or delis in the lobbies and employees are expected to take their lunch breaks there, where they are available if needed and don't have to leave the premises for long periods of time. Other offices make a habit of taking group orders and ordering food in on a daily basis. You may find that your office mates bring their lunch from home every day and eat at their desks. Or, you may find that lunch breaks are a social occasion, where groups of people from the office head to the latest eatery for an hour of eating and hanging out. Your office may even have a great break room that's fully equipped for cooking and storing food and where everyone eats at different times throughout the day.

Because eating is often a social occasion, the lunch hour can be important to your work relationships. If everyone in your department always goes out together for lunch, but you decline their invitation every day, you may come across as anti-social. On the other hand, if you and a few of your coworkers make a habit of going to lunch together regularly but don't extend invitations to others in the office, it may result in hurt feelings.

The quick break

Eight or more hours makes for a long day and sometimes one lunch break just doesn't cut it. That's where the quick 10- or 15-minute break comes in. You won't hear a bell going off indicating that it's time to take your scheduled mid-morning break, but taking one or two short breaks a day is usually fine in most office environments.

Taking a few minutes away from a tedious project to go outside and enjoy a nice day can be great for productivity by renewing your energy and enthusiasm for work. Many productivity experts even suggest taking a minute or two every hour to get up from your desk, do a few stretches, laugh with a coworker, or just walk to get a drink of water. Make sure you use these breaks wisely and that your supervisor agrees they are important.

The smoke break

More problematic these days is the smoke break. Once commonplace in working life, the smoke break used to be a time for coworkers to commiserate and relax from the stress of the workday. However, smoking is now considered a bad habit and is discouraged in most workplaces.

If you have a smoking habit, you must be sure to handle it with courtesy and discretion. Find out where you are allowed to smoke in the perimeter of the office building. Some buildings have special smoking "tents" or awnings where employees are allowed to smoke. Others require that smokers be a certain distance away from the building. Be sure not to litter the front of your office building with discarded butts; most buildings will provide a receptacle in which you can dispose of them. Keep your smoke breaks to a minimum; let someone know where you will be and when you will be back, and try your best not to let the smell of smoke follow you back into the office.

Most importantly, don't give the impression of abusing your employer's break policy. Non-smokers will resent that you are taking extra time off and it won't win you any points with management, either.

The annoying coworker

Chews with his mouth open. Makes a funny snorting, sniffling, throat-clearing sound all the time. Complains about everything. Sound familiar? Every office has at least one annoying coworker. Irritation is inevitable in a work environment. Here's an overview of the most common annoyances at work:

The Interrupter. She or he interrupts people while they are working, talking, or in the middle of something important.

The Loudmouth. He or she talks loudly while on the phone, slams doors, has loud conversations, clears his or her throat loudly and regularly. This person basically makes loud and/or distracting noises on a regular basis.

The Helpless Wonder. He or she fakes helplessness to get out of doing work. This person can't—or won't—learn how to do simple tasks (like fixing copier paper jams, for example) because he or she knows that someone else will do them instead.

The Germ. This coworker comes to work and spreads the wealth—of his or her germs. People think they are showing their dedication when they stick out a day at work while battling the flu, but nothing could be farther from the truth. Going to work ill and getting everyone else sick doesn't help anyone or prove anything.

The Salesperson. This person sees colleagues as potential dollar signs; he or she will try to sell you Avon, Amway, and other products for profit. Nobody wants to be pressured to buy something they don't want at the workplace.

Mr. or Ms. Home-Away-From-Home. This person does stuff at work that should be done at home. This includes downloading music, making calls to plan his/her wedding, shopping online for gifts and even more personal activities like flossing or clipping his/her nails. (Believe it or not, people actually do these things!)

The Flake. This person is chronically late, unprepared, disorganized and full of excuses.

The Oversharer (aka, Mr. or Ms. TMI). Some people share everything, from the details of their children's diapers to, well, everything. Not in good form.

The Klepto. This person might be well-meaning, but he or she borrows stuff and doesn't return it.

The Grump. This colleague would rather complain than work proactively to address problems or make changes.

So what to do about it? First of all, make sure you aren't the culprit. Second, try to ignore it. Everyone is annoying at least once in a while, and modern life has given us all shorter fuses. Don't be too quick to judge. However, if annoying behaviors go beyond just annoying and start to affect productivity or workplace morale, they must be addressed. A first line of defense is just to be honest and let the person know that what he/she is doing is, well, annoying. (Of course, you'd want to say so in more diplomatic terms.) If that doesn't remedy the situation, it's best to take it up with a supervisor or the human resources department.

Office politics

Office politics: every workplace has its share, and it's not all bad. In fact, in order to achieve career success, you must learn to master a certain amount of office politics. Here's how.

By definition, politics is dealing with people in a way that produces outcomes that are beneficial to you. Nothing wrong with that, right? Right – as long as the playing field is even and people conduct themselves with integrity. Unfortunately, this isn't always the case. The bad news is that in your work life you will come across people who brown nose, lie, take credit for work they didn't do, and are generally unsavory characters. The good news is that most people are good, fair people who want the same things that you do: to earn a living while learning and growing as a person, being recognized for a job well done, helping others and having a little fun along the way.

The best news is that to become a pro at office politicking, you don't have to do much more than be a good person. Following are essential tips for succeeding in office politics:

Develop a genuine interest in other people. If you are really interested in other people's experiences, opinions, and perspectives, they will respond in kind.

Develop a healthy curiosity about the world. Curiosity leads to growth, learning, and a more well-rounded experience.

Be empathetic. Half of being a successful office "politician" is understanding what other people want and need.

Be a good listener. Developing good listening skills is key to making meaningful connections with people at work.

Make time for other people. It's tempting to think that keeping your head down and putting your nose to the grindstone is the best way to get ahead at work, but that's not always the case. While hard work is appreciated and rewarded, you also have to be likeable and interesting, demonstrate good character, and show that you care about other people in order to achieve career success. All of this is hard to do if you don't take the time to get to know your colleagues – and, yes, participate in a little office politics.

Be true to yourself. You shouldn't have to be someone else to be successful in office politics.

Be positive, respectful and considerate. Act like the person you want to work with.

Office politics pitfalls

As essential as it is, office politics isn't always pretty. The truth is it can be downright ugly, but don't think that you have to lower yourself to the lowest common denominator. As comedienne Lily Tomlin famously said, "The problem with the rat race is that even if you win, you're still a rat." By recognizing the most common office politics pitfalls and employing some simple strategies to avoid them, you can sidestep problems and keep your career on track.

Cliques. It's human nature – people with similar interests or experience tend to group together. It's no different at work. There's nothing wrong with developing groups of friends at the office, until it leads to the exclusion of others, hurt feelings, and bad morale.

Do what you can to avoid closing yourself off in a clique. Invite co-workers to join you and your friends for lunch, make sure that everyone is always in on the conversation and the joke, and don't give anyone special treatment at the office just because they are your friend. And if you find that you are on the outside of an office clique, don't sweat it. Do your best to be friendly, courteous, and helpful to everyone you work with. Work friendships and alliances will develop naturally and fairly.

Gossip. Unfortunately, gossip is all but unavoidable in the workplace. The office grapevine is a staple of modern office life, and does serve its purpose. If not wildly speculative, malicious, or untrue, gossip can be a relatively harmless way to bond with coworkers and spread fun and positive news. For example, telling your office mate that Eric from the IT department got engaged over the weekend and looks really happy is, by most definitions, gossip. But it's also harmless. On the other hand, repeating that you heard Eric's getting divorced—and all the unsavory details related to the break up—is harmful. At its worst, gossip can hurt feelings, lower morale, and even damage or destroy careers. And you don't have to be the subject of gossip to be harmed by it: earning a reputation as an office gossip means you appear disloyal, untrustworthy, superficial, or dishonest in the eyes of colleagues and supervisors.

The best way to figure out if you are repeating harmless news or spreading potentially hurtful gossip is to evaluate your motivation behind repeating it. If your motive is to promote yourself, get attention, or to be the center of attention, you are gossiping. Ask yourself this: How would the subject of this news feel if he or she heard me repeating the news. To be truly gossip-free, you have to stop gossip in its tracks – and refuse to listen to it too. If someone starts repeating gossip to you, simply stop them and let them know that you are uncomfortable with the subject matter.

How to deal with dirty politics
Favoritism, back stabbing, sabotage and other nasty office behavior. From time to time you will encounter people in your career who are dishonest, unfair, unscrupulous or just plain mean. We all want to consider our coworkers friends, but what to do if you become the object of a coworker's dirty politics?

You don't have to just take it if you are being affected by favoritism, coworker sabotage, gossip, or backstabbing. By using a few simple strategies, you can rise above the drama and stay on course:

Develop a paper trail as a precaution. Always keep meticulous records of your office communications and work. That way, if a coworker tries to accuse you of falling behind on work, or a supervisor unfairly claims to have passed you over for a prime assignment because the quality of your work is poor, you can respond with confidence by using your arsenal of proof to the contrary.

Don't suffer in silence. The squeaky wheel gets the grease. If colleagues are unfairly trying to undermine your career or one-up you, making your accomplishments and value known is a great counter-strategy. Make sure your boss knows about your successes and strengths.

Take the high road. It's never a good policy to roll in the mud with your enemies. If you are the target of dirty office politics, rise above it by staying calm, focusing on the positive, and proactively – and fairly – addressing the problem. Don't let what is going on affect your job performance or your confidence – that's exactly what the saboteur wants.

Learn to communicate. Sometimes, simple communication is the answer. Speaking calmly and directly to the person who is at the root of the problem can go a long way to solving personality conflicts. Honest and open communication can help you understand your coworker's perspective, and may even make your coworker aware of how his or her behavior is affecting you.

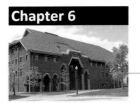

Chapter 6

TIPS FOR BUSINESS-RELATED FUNCTIONS

Never put the napkin in your lap (in Latvia). Lower your eyes when introduced to someone who is older or has more status than you (in Nigeria). Use both hands to present your business card (in Sri Lanka). Keep your elbows on the table. Keep your elbows off the table. Slurp your soup. Never slurp your soup. International etiquette can just about give a person whiplash. In some countries, you're expected to enter a conference room in order of status. In others, you don't talk about business at all during the first meeting.

Why are meetings, meals, and other business-related functions so highly ritualized in many countries? Even though the rules vary—from country to country and even from organization to organization—they all allow a way to show respect. In this chapter we'll cover the etiquette of business-related functions in the United States.

Business meetings

In many organizations, when you're not in a meeting you're planning for the next one. According to a study by the Wharton Center for Applied Research, some U.S. workers spend as much as 23 hours a week in meetings. What's more, most managers say that only 56 percent of meetings are productive! Get the most out of meetings by following these tips:

If you are leading the meeting...

- First, ask yourself if a meeting is the best way to accomplish your objectives. If the purpose is simply to share information or provoke a discussion on a single topic, email or wiki might be more efficient.

- Set an agenda and send it to everyone who will attend the meeting ahead of time. Consult with meeting participants to see if there are items they would like to add to the agenda.

- Notify participants as early as possible so the meeting won't inordinately interrupt their day.

- Inform all presenters and contributors know about their role in the meeting in advance.

- Select a meeting room big enough to accommodate everyone and make sure there is enough seating.

- If the meeting is large and not everyone will know each other, consider using name tags.

- Start and end the meeting on time – it shows respect for other people's time and ensures that everyone will be able to attend the entire meeting.

- Begin by making necessary introductions, then by summarizing the purpose of the meeting and the points to be covered.

- Consider creating some ground rules for the meeting. For example, participants will want to know how decisions will be made: Majority rule? Committee?

- Stay focused and on topic.

- Create an action sheet for the meeting to distribute to everyone as a follow up. This action sheet should include a brief summary of the meeting, agreed-upon items for further action, and the time, date and location of the next meeting, if there is to be one.

- Finally, evaluate the success of the meeting and ask for others' input. This will help you to run an even better meeting the next time around.

If you are participating in a meeting...

- Let those running the meeting know if you will attend as soon as possible.

- Arrive on time.

- Be prepared. Bring all necessary materials and review the agenda ahead of time.

- Stay on topic and don't bring up irrelevant points or subjects that will cause the discussion to drift.

- Don't interrupt.

- Participate. Show interest and involvement in the discussion by making comments and asking questions.

- Take notes.

- If asked, give the meeting leader constructive input on what went well and how the meeting could have been even better.

Business meals

In some organizations, business meals are a common way to entertain clients, develop professional relationships, or conduct meetings. While the etiquette depends on the situation, there are some rules that apply to all business meals.

When you host a business meal...

- Make sure you are prepared, organized and polished.

- Invite guests as early as possible so that they'll be likely to attend and stay for the duration of the meeting.

- Always make reservations in advance and confirm the reservations a day before the event. Choose a restaurant that you are confident will provide good service, good food, and offer a menu that will satisfy everyone.

- Arrive at the restaurant early so that you can communicate with restaurant staff, arrange for payment of the bill, make sure the table is appropriate, and greet guests. Note: If you must be late, contact the restaurant to let them know that your guests should be seated and offered drinks and appetizers. Try to contact your guests as well to apologize for your delay.

- Do not order until all the guests have arrived. Place your order after all guests have placed theirs.

- Allow your guests to choose their place at the table, and offer them the preferred seating, such as the seat with the view of the window or at the head of the table.

- If you have not arranged for payment ahead of time, arrange for the bill to be delivered to you at the end of the meal. Always pay for business meals that you have hosted.

- Thank your guests for attending.

- Tip the servers well (20% is standard) and thank the restaurant manager if the service was exceptional. A good restaurant and restaurant staff that you can rely on to support your important business meals is a great asset.

- If necessary, follow up business meals with an email, memo, or call to summarize the business that was conducted during the meal and remind attendees of action items.

When you are the guest at a business meal, follow these tips:

- Be sure to RSVP as soon as possible.

- Be prepared: Read over the agenda and gather any materials you'll need.

- If you have special dietary needs, let the host know. For example, if you have a seafood allergy, your host will want to know that so he or she doesn't schedule the meeting at a seafood restaurant.

- Arrive on time. If you must be late, try to contact your host. At the very least, contact the restaurant to have a staff member pass on a message to your host that you will be late.

- Wait to sit at the table until your host indicates that you should be seated.

- Avoid ordering the most expensive item on the menu.

- If the bill for the meal is placed in front of you by accident, wait for the host to correct the mistake. If the host does not make an attempt to correct the mistake, offer to split the expense. Always come prepared to split the expense for the meal.

- Always thank your host for his/her hospitality.

GOOD TO KNOW

A great source for learningabout international etiquette:
www.kwintessential.co.uk/

Dining etiquette
Here are some reminders about standard dining etiquette:

- During the meal, keep your cell phone off or program it to vibrate.

- Wait to pick up the menu until the host picks up his or hers.

- Immediately after being seated, remove your napkin from the table, unfold it, and place it in your lap.

- Never crumple your napkin, shake it out, or use it as a bib.

- If your napkin falls on the floor, don't pick it up. Instead, ask your server for a new one.

- If you get up during the meal, place your napkin on your chair, not on the table.

- Do not rest your elbows or arms on the table while eating.

- Excuse yourself to the restroom if you must apply cosmetics or take medicine.

- Do not send food back unless it is inedible. If you must send food back, be as discreet and polite as possible.

- Never place used utensils on the table or tablecloth. Instead rest them on the edge of your plate. The knife should rest on the back edge, while the fork and spoon should rest on the sides.

- Bring your food to your mouth, not your mouth to the food.

- Never blow on your food to cool it off.

- Chew with your mouth closed and never speak with your mouth full of food.

- Do not double dip in communal foods, such as appetizer dips.

- Do not scrape your plate.

- Only use your hands to handle food when appropriate – when eating sandwiches or berries, for example. If food falls off your plate onto the table, pick it up with your utensils and place it on the edge of your plate.

- Never pick up items that fall onto the floor. Instead, ask for assistance from your server.

- When eating soup, place your spoon into the soup along the bowl edge closest to you. Move the spoon toward the opposite edge until it is about two-thirds full. Lift the spoon from the bowl and rub the bottom of the spoon on the inside edge to avoid any drips. Sip the soup from the spoon – never slurp it. Never lift your soup bowl.

- Never hold a knife in your hand while eating. You should cut enough food for one or two bites at a time, place the knife on the top rim of your plate, then eat the pieces you have prepared.

- Try to eat at the same pace as the other guests.

- If you suspect that you have food in your teeth, excuse yourself and attend to it in the restroom.

- To inform your server that you have finished your meal, place your fork and knife next to each other diagonally across your plate (from the 4 o'clock to 11 o'clock position with the sharp edge of the knife facing away from you).

- After finishing your meal, place your napkin to the left of your plate, unfolded.

The place setting

The place setting for a meal can be intimidating, so we'll cover the basics here. You'd need more detailed protocol for, say, a luncheon with the Queen of England, but this should cover most situations you're likely to encounter. A diagram of a semi-formal place setting has been provided at the end of this section for your review.

- A simple way to remember the layout of a place setting is that all utensils to the right of the plate (besides the knife) are for drinking. All the utensils to the left of the plate are for eating.

- If you are ever unsure of what utensil to use when eating or drinking, wait for your host or other guests to begin and then follow their lead.

- As you begin your meal, use the outermost fork or spoon first and work your way in towards the service plate with each course.

- Never place used utensils on the table or tablecloth. Instead, place them on the outer edge of your plate. The knife should rest on the back edge of the plate and the fork and spoon should rest on the sides. When preparing coffee or tea, place the teaspoon on the saucer.

- Depending on the restaurant, the dessert utensils may or may not be present during the initial part of the meal. In some cases, these utensils are only presented once dessert has been ordered. However, in a formal situation, or when a prearranged meal is being served, guests are aware that dessert will be served by the placement of a dessert fork and spoon located horizontally above the plate. Before dessert is served, the server will clear any remaining utensils and food from your dining area and move the dessert fork and spoon into their appropriate positions.

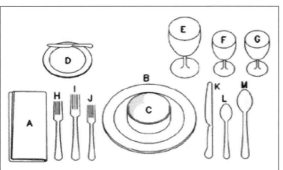

A = Napkin
B = Service Plate
C = Soup Bowl on a Linear Plate
D = Bread & Butter Plate with Butter Knife
E = Water Glass
F = Wine Glass (Red)
G = Wine Glass (White)
H = Salad Fork
I = Dinner Fork
J = Dessert Fork
K = Knife
L = Teaspoon
M = Soup Spoon

Not sure which bread plate or drinking glasses are yours?

TIP

Make an "okay" sign with both of your hands.

The left hand thumb and pointer finger make a lower case "**b**". This reminds you that your bread plate is to the left of your place setting. The right hand thumb and pointer finger make a lower case "**d**". This reminds you that your drinking glasses are to th e right of your place setting.

Other important dining tips to remember

Here are a few more important tips to keep in mind before you venture into the sometimes murky waters of the business meal:

- Review your company's policies regarding the use of alcohol during business functions. If your company does not have a policy, consult your supervisor.

- If your host asks if you would like a cocktail and you are not sure if anyone else will be ordering one, request water or soda. You can always order a cocktail later.

- Never feel obliged to order alcohol or to explain yourself if you abstain.

- Know your limits when it comes to alcohol and stick to them! A few drinks are not worth losing your job or compromising your credibility or integrity with your colleagues and supervisors.

- Conversation is important at a business meal – be outgoing and engaging even if you're dying to get back to the office to complete a project.

- Delay discussing business until everyone has ordered so that everyone can participate and direct his/her full attention to the business at hand.

- Complete the meal before presenting any documents.

- A restaurant is not an ideal location to discuss sensitive business subjects. You never know who is within earshot.

- Always treat restaurant staff with respect; the way you treat those who serve you is often a good indication of your character.

Staff retreats

Staff retreats are gatherings in a relaxed setting. The main goal of a staff retreat is often team building, though it's also a time to share ideas, reflect on experiences, discuss business issues, learn new skills, and set goals. Retreats can be as simple as a day-long event at a local conference center, or as elaborate as a week-long, vacation-like event at a resort destination. Here are some tips for making the most of a staff retreat:

- Be prepared. Know what will be discussed and what will be expected of you ahead of time so you can prepare yourself and organize materials.

- View the retreat as an opportunity to get to know your coworkers better, grow as an employee, and learn about your organization's goals, mission and future.

- Participate! Your organization's leadership has planned the retreat because they want it to be productive and they believe it will be helpful. No matter how silly the activity may seem, it can't hurt to participate. You may learn something new, build a better relationship with a colleague or supervisor, or get an important issue out into the open.

Office parties

It's the stuff that urban legend is made of – the office holiday party. Who can forget the story of the manager who started breakdancing after a few vodka tonics? Or the vice president who dominated the karaoke station? Throughout your career, you will be invited – or perhaps even required – to attend a range of office celebrations from holiday parties and summer picnics to award ceremonies and retirement parties. Make sure you don't become the stuff of office lore by following these recommendations for office celebrations.

- Remember that although office parties are social events, they are still business events, too. Behave professionally and as if you are being observed every minute.

- Attend, if only for a while. Turning down invitations to business social functions can make you appear ungrateful or anti-social.

- Spend at least 30 minutes at the party but don't overstay your welcome by partying until the early morning hours.

- Dress appropriately. Skip anything too revealing, gimmicky, or flashy.

- Don't spend the entire time talking business. It's boring, even for people who are also in the organization.

- Avoid controversial subjects, such as religion, politics, and off-color jokes.

- Keep your drink in your left hand, so you are not offering people a cold, wet handshake.

- If you do drink, know your limits.

- Use the time to build or strengthen relationships with people you may not see regularly, such as top management, people from other departments, and employees from other locations. Don't spend the whole time talking with your office mate or best friend.

- Remember that friends or significant others are not always on the guest list for office parties. If guests are permitted, make sure you bring one who will represent you well.

- Remember to thank the person responsible for planning and coordinating the party. Sending a thank-you note or email to top management for hosting the party is a nice touch as well.

- If you are drinking, make sure you make arrangements for getting home safely.

Social events outside the office

From time to time, you will be with supervisors and colleagues in social settings beyond the office walls. For instance, you might play golf or another sport with coworkers, participate in the same club or church, take classes at the local university, or attend mutual friends' weddings and other celebrations.

To be prepared for these situations, remember:

- Never pretend that you don't see the other person, no matter how much you might want to. Chances are he or she will notice and be angry, hurt, or both.

- When greeting your colleague, introduce yourself immediately by name – it's easy for people to have problems recognizing others out of context or on the spur of the moment. Don't be upset or embarrassed if a colleague doesn't remember your name or doesn't seem to recognize you at first – just realize that he/she was taken by surprise.

- Always introduce everyone in your party to your colleague.

- If you have had too much to drink or are in the company of a friend or family member who you fear might say too much or do something unbecoming, greet your colleague and be friendly, but excuse yourself as quickly as possible.

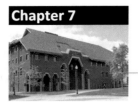

Chapter 7

WORKPLACE CHALLENGES AND SITUATIONS

Experience and failure are great teachers, and you don't even need to take out a student loan to benefit from their lessons. No matter how prepared or skilled, no matter how good our intentions, we're bound to make mistakes or deal with work-related mental or emotional challenges. Will you fail occasionally? Yep. Will you say the wrong thing at the wrong time to the wrong person? Probably. Will you feel stressed and overwhelmed? Likely. There are some things you can do to prevent these issues, but there will be times when you, well, are presented with the opportunity to learn from your mistakes.

This chapter covers tips that can help you gracefully tackle the challenges you may face in your career, from making mistakes to feeling burned out.

Making mistakes

The question is not, "Will I make mistakes?" but rather, "How can I deal with mistakes once I've made them?" Successful people learn from their missteps and bounce back. A professional who handles his or her mistakes well will learn resilience and gain valuable experience. Here's how to fail well:

Be accountable. Own up to your mistakes immediately. Don't hope that no one will notice or that it will somehow go away if you ignore it. The longer you wait to accept responsibility, the worse the situation is likely to get.

Apologize, but don't make excuses. A sincere apology is necessary, but a litany of why the mistake was made or why it wasn't your fault will make a bad impression.

Learn from the mistake. Evaluate what you did wrong, how you handled the situation, and what you can do differently next time to avoid the same snafu.

Avoid careless mistakes. You are going to make mistakes no matter how hard you try not to, so take care to avoid making careless ones.

Don't beat yourself up. You've made a mistake, you've dealt with it the best you can – now forgive yourself and move on. There's nothing to be gained by dwelling on your mistake or becoming angry. Remember that at some point the mistake will be five days ago, five months ago, a year ago, three years ago, etc. Will it seem like that big of a deal when you look back at it from those vantage points?

Embarrassment

Embarrassment is not fatal, but sometimes it feels that way. It's awkward and unpleasant at best, I-want-to-crawl-into-a-cave at worst. But, like taxes, death, and political scandals, it's part of life. If you do or say something embarrassing (or someone else does), you can't go back in time and change it, but there are things you can do to minimize the negative impact of the moment.

Maintain your composure. By maintaining control and acting confident and respectful, you will show others that you are not easily shaken. If it's not possible to maintain your composure, excuse yourself so you can deal with your emotions in private.

Avoid drawing attention to other people's embarrassment. If someone else embarrasses him or herself, do what you can to divert attention from the situation and minimize the embarrassment. However, if the person tries to use humor to diffuse the situation, laugh with him or her.

Don't linger on the situation. Everyone knows what it feels like to be embarrassed and will probably try to do what they can to help you recover. If you need to apologize, do so but don't draw the process out so much that it makes others uncomfortable. If you don't need to apologize, just regain your composure and move on.

Boredom

At times, you may find that you are bored at work. Being bored from time to time isn't a big problem, but if you have lost your overall enthusiasm and passion for your job and find yourself settled into a mundane and uninteresting routine, your boredom might negatively affect your job performance. Worse, it could make you feel dissatisfied and unchallenged. Try the following to alleviate your boredom:

Break up mundane tasks with exciting ones. If you spend days on end filing, you are bound to get bored. If possible, file for a few minutes every day and spend the rest of your day on the more interesting and creative aspects of your job.

Volunteer for new projects. Even if it is something as small as volunteering to plan the office holiday party or joining a committee, adding new responsibilities and challenges to your daily routine can add new dimension to your work day. Plus, you might find that you have undiscovered talents or interests.

Discuss your situation with your boss. You might not want to use the word "bored." But do let him or her know that you are available to take on new challenges and interested in trying new things.

Consider a change. If you've tried everything and still find that you are bored with your job, you may need to seek employment that is more challenging and better suited to your skills and talents.

Motivation

In the early days of your career, motivation is not usually a problem. A new job! A paycheck! All sorts of stuff to learn and people to meet! But as time goes on you might experience a temporary rut or find yourself losing passion and motivation. Here are some things you can do to boost your attitude:

Add fun and variety to your work routine. Change things up, whether it's the way you approach tasks or your lunchtime routine. Branch out and make more social connections with coworkers. Challenge yourself to vary your workday.

Seek leadership roles at your organization. Leading projects and people will give you a sense of purpose.

Concentrate on your goals and the big picture. Remind yourself how your work – no matter how mundane or boring – is contributing to the mission of your organization and helping you to develop valuable skills and experience.

Seek feedback from supervisors and colleagues. Positive feedback will make you feel good; constructive criticism will help you set goals.

Cultivate a positive outlook. Notice everything you're accomplishing. Notice the things that make your workplace good. Take time to connect with those coworkers who are interesting and inspiring.

Handling criticism

Some people make a career out of being the lightning rods for criticism. For most of us, however, it's a necessary but sometimes unpleasant part of the job. Learning how to handle criticism objectively and professionally is important.

Listen. As you are receiving criticism, don't interrupt. Let the person finish to make sure you get all of the information.

Stay calm. Keeping your cool will give you the emotional and mental space to figure out the best way to respond. On the other hand, getting angry or defensive will probably escalate the situation and make you appear too volatile.

Make sure you understand. Confirm what you have heard to make sure you got all of the points.

Seek privacy. Being criticized in public is not acceptable. If you find yourself in this situation, calmly ask the person if you can continue the situation somewhere private. If the person refuses, you may have to consider cutting the conversation short and continuing later in private.

Consider the criticism. Ultimately, there are two things to deal with when you've been criticized: the manner and the message. If someone criticizes you harshly and in public, it's much more likely to trigger a defensive response, even if the criticism could ultimately help you. Take time to reflect on the situation and determine which parts of the criticism were valid. Also, reflect on the interaction: what went well and what didn't? How would you respond to a similar situation in the future?

Stress

Stress can be positive. For instance, it can motivate us and drive us to find new and better ways of doing things. However, if stress becomes overwhelming it can wreak havoc on your physical and emotional well-being, not to mention your work performance. The symptoms of stress include

Physical: Experiencing weight loss or gain, headaches, fatigue, changes in sleep patterns, stomach problems, muscle aches, and tightness.

Emotional: Feeling easily angered or frustrated; experiencing nervousness, irritability, and mood swings.

Mental: Feeling confused, demonstrating a lack of interest in favorite activities, loss of concentration, and forgetfulness.

You will have your fair share of stress in your job. Ultimately, the way you manage it will depend on your situation and your personality. Here are some ways to reign in your stress:

Identify your stressors. Determine what stresses you out so you can deal with it. Hate being late? Make sure you plan more than enough time to do everything. Freak out when you have to give reports at meetings? Take a public speaking class.

Manage your time. A lot of stress results from not having enough time to complete tasks. Keep a calendar and a running to-do list to help you manage your time, and make sure that you fairly assess how much time it will take you to complete something – then add 15 minutes to account for unplanned interruptions.

Organize. A lot of stress also results from disorganization. When you can't find things, don't have set systems for dealing with situations, and are generally disorganized, you add a lot of unnecessary stress to your life.

Prioritize. Decide what is really important and what can wait.

Ask for help. Learn to ask for assistance or delegate.

Say no. It's difficult early in your career to say no, but it's important to take on only those things you know you can do and do them well.

Avoid procrastination. Set deadlines and stick to them.

Take time for yourself. Take breaks when necessary throughout the day, take vacations, and fill your nights and weekends with things you enjoy, like hobbies and friends.

Keep your perspective. When you are feeling really stressed, take a step back and ask yourself how the situation will really affect you or others. Will you lose your job? Will someone be harmed? Will it affect your life for years to come? Probably not. In fact, in two months you will most likely have forgotten all about it. Putting things in perspective is an instant stress reliever.

Create a strong support network. Having friends, mentors and supporter is important to handling stress. Vent, get advice, laugh—don't feel alone in your stress.

Get professional guidance. If you feel that your stress is out of control, you may need professional help in learning to deal with it. Seeing a counselor is one option, but you may also consider taking a class in meditation or taking a seminar in stress reduction.

Burnout

Burnout is serious emotional exhaustion resulting from your job. It's not uncommon – most people experience it at some time during their career – but it can be serious. People who have job burnout lose interest in their jobs, stop giving their best effort to their work, often experience emotional and physical turmoil that affects their quality of life, and may even end up losing their jobs. If you suspect you may be experiencing job burnout, ask yourself the following questions:

- Do you dread going to work?
- Do you find yourself longing for Friday night all week long and feel a sense of dread on Sunday afternoons because you know you must return to work the next day?
- Do you do the bare minimum at work and just coast along, but still feel drained at the end of the day?
- Are you experiencing health problems like headaches, stomachaches, and fatigue?
- Do you feel irritable, moody, and resentful when it comes to work?
- Do you find that you no longer enjoy parts of your job that used to be a pleasure?
- Are you jealous and resentful toward people who claim to love their job?
- Do you lose your temper easily?

If you can answer yes to one or more of these questions, you may be on the track to job burnout.

People who work under a lot of job stress, are fearful of losing their job, work with a toxic supervisor or coworkers, or are working at a company undergoing a lot of change or turmoil (layoffs, bankruptcy or scandal, for example) are prime candidates for job burnout. But burnout can happen to anyone. Here's how to deal with it:

Admit it. If you are feeling burned out, admit it so you can take the steps to fix it. Pretending that everything is okay will just make things worse.

Take care of yourself. Eat right, get enough sleep, exercise, and see a doctor regularly. Feeling unhealthy can contribute to job burnout or make it worse.

Nurture your relationships at work and beyond. Having a strong support system of coworkers, friends, and family can help you cope with the stresses of your job.

Take a break. Make sure you use your vacation time, take sick days when you aren't well, and take regular breaks throughout the day to do something you enjoy.

Draw the line. Burnout often occurs when a person doesn't know how to stop working. Make a commitment that you will not take work home with you on a regular basis, that you won't check your email at midnight, that you will turn your cell phone off after a certain time, and that you will begin to set limits on how much you are willing to give and do at work. Work can't be your entire life.

Make time for fun. Whether it's planning a fun Friday lunch for coworkers, forwarding a great joke to your office mates, or planning activities for the weekends, take time to laugh.

Communicate. Let your supervisors and coworkers know, in a positive way, that you are making changes to help you refocus on your work. Find someone you can vent to and use as a sounding board.

Prioritize. Be realistic about what you can accomplish and decide what is really important to you and what things you can let slide—both at work and at home.

Reclaim your power by making a plan. You are not powerless over your work or your life. Set goals and make a plan for how you will create the kind of work life you want. Maybe this includes more education, a new position, a different focus, or a new job.

Face that it might be time to move on. Burnout doesn't necessarily mean that you are in the wrong career, the wrong position, or at the wrong company—but it can. If you have come to realize that you have chosen a career that is all wrong for you, that your position doesn't fit you or your skills at all, or that your company has a culture that doesn't fit with your values, get out. Make a plan for moving on—and then do it.

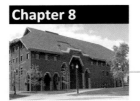

Chapter 8

WORKING WITH AND
FOR YOUR BOSS

Filmmakers and screenwriters have a lot of fun portraying bosses who are ineffectual at best and crazy at worst. Real life is, as usual, more complicated. Some bosses will be inspiring and motivating, others will be enigmatic. All of them will have their quirks, but the same could be said for anyone in any organization.

Your relationship with your boss is central to your professional development. Their importance in our lives may be why they occupy such a mythic role in the movies. Relationships with bosses, however, are like any relationship: they require mutual respect, communication, compromise, honesty, and work to develop and maintain over time.

This chapter will discuss how you can develop a good relationship with your boss and how to use that relationship to grow professionally.

Develop a good relationship with your boss

There are many things you can't control when it comes to developing a good relationship with your boss. Your organization's culture will to a large extent determine your relationship, as will your and your boss's personalities. However, there are some things you can do to maintain a good relationship:

Demonstrate respect. This is obvious, and the same could be said for any person you work with, but it's so fundamental it's worth stating. The more you demonstrate respect for your boss and others in the organization, the better your working life will be.

Be honest. If your boss asks for feedback, give it to him or her. If there's a problem, admit it. And if you make a mistake, own up to it as soon as you can.

Give your boss fair notice. If you want to plan a vacation, need time off for illness, or may experience problems being on time due to family responsibilities, let your boss know. She or he may be very understanding, and at the very least will appreciate your candor so that she or he can make plans for your absence. This goes for your resignation as well. Even though your boss may not be your boss for long, she or he may be willing to serve as a useful reference or mentor. Give your boss fair advance notice of your departure to keep the relationship friendly.

Maintain boundaries. You want to have a great relationship with your boss, but you don't have to be best friends. Don't share very personal information or invite him/her to be your friend on Facebook. Your boss is still your boss, no matter how strong your relationship is – and she or he may have to make unpopular or difficult decisions.

Be positive. Make it clear that you bring ideas and solutions to the organizations, not complaints.

Manage your emotions. You don't have to be a robot, but keep your emotions in check and avoid letting your feelings get the best of you around your boss.

Take constructive criticism well. Your boss is there to manage you, which means helping you develop professionally and grow as an employee. Part of this job requires criticism of your work. Don't be defensive; keep an open mind and use the criticism to improve.

Manage yourself

You might have a boss who micro-manages your work, or one who leaves a few general instructions before he or she heads off to yet another conference. No matter what kind of supervision you receive from your boss, there are certain things you should do to make sure you succeed at your job:

Always restate your boss's expectations and concerns out loud to confirm that you understand your task.

Gather as much information as possible from your boss at the start of a project. Ask lots of questions, confirm expectations, deadlines and consequences, and make sure you understand everything completely.

Take notes. When you take good notes you'll be able to refer to them later and can avoid asking unnecessary questions.

Try to anticipate your boss's questions and concerns and address them immediately. This will foster your boss's confidence in your ability to do the job and put her or his mind at ease.

Provide regular, concise feedback to your boss on your progress.

Make sure to keep impeccable records of all of your work. That way, if necessary, you will be able to provide documentation of your work and justification for your decisions.

Be as independent as possible. Critique your own work. Find other resources besides your boss that can help you complete your work – coworkers, documents, books, Web sites, etc.

Monitor your own progress. If your boss doesn't provide you with deadlines, set them for yourself so you have the structure necessary to stay on task.

Make connections with others in the organization. Develop relationships with coworkers and other managers that you can rely on for guidance, advice and feedback.

Take advantage of every opportunity you are given to improve yourself.
Let your boss know you are interested in training seminars, extra projects, or other learning and growth experiences. Doing so will not only help you in your current position, it could also be great experience to include on your resume.

Toot your own horn (within reason). If necessary, make sure your boss knows when you put in the extra effort or go the extra mile, like working late or over the weekend.

Handling and resolving conflicts

From time to time, you and your boss will not see eye to eye. Occasional conflicts with your boss aren't the end of the world; in fact, learning how to handle these conflicts is an important learning experience and can actually lead to a closer and more productive relationship with your boss. To constructively deal with conflict between you and your boss:

Pick your battles. Make sure what you are upset about is really worth pursuing.

Address problems as they occur. Don't sit and stew. If something is bothering you, or you suspect that something is bothering your boss, address it right away.

Have an honest discussion. Request a meeting with your boss. Find out what's expected of you and how you can meet those expectations – especially in relation to the specific conflict you are having. Getting feedback may be all you need.

Keep records. Keep a meticulous record of all of your work – emails, phone calls, client interactions, documents, reports, etc. If your boss has a problem with your work or accuses you of something that is not true, you will have the evidence to back up your claims.

Control yourself. Yelling, crying, or generally making a scene is never effective. It's unprofessional and makes you look like a loose cannon.

Look for support. If you are having a specific problem with your boss or just have problems with her in general, look to a coworker or mentor for guidance. An unbiased, outside opinion may help you put the problem in perspective or give you the input you need to develop a strategy to deal with it. Others at your company might also know added history or motivation for your boss's behavior. Just make sure you conduct yourself professionally and never reduce yourself to gossiping about the boss or criticizing him or her to someone who may leak the information.

Know your rights. Employees have rights and you don't have to put up with behavior that violates your rights, is over the top, or is generally offensive. If you know your rights, you will know when they've been violated—and what recourse you have. The U.S. Equal Employment Opportunity Commission (www.eeoc.gov) is a good starting place if you have questions about your rights.

Go to the top. If the problem is extreme, you may have to talk to your boss's boss, or a representative from human resources. Just make sure that the problem truly warrants this extreme action.

You'll learn a lot—both professionally and personally—from all the bosses you encounter in your career. Some bosses will be excellent mentors and others might teach other, inadvertent lessons about interpersonal relationships.

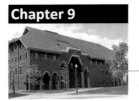

Chapter 9

COWORKERS

Eight hours a day, five days a week…some quick calculations reveal that you could spend up to 2,000 hours a year with your coworkers. Will they be your best friends? Maybe. Will one be your future spouse? Maybe. Will your relationship with them determine your job satisfaction and productivity? Absolutely.

Research shows that, after several years on the job, many people count their relationships with coworkers as their closest and most satisfying. It makes sense that we'd be drawn to the people we work with. First, we spend a great deal of time with them. Second, we have a shared experience of working with the same people in the same environment. Third, we tend to work for organizations that reflect our values, which means our coworkers usually share those values.

This chapter will discuss office friendships, office romances, and dealing with difficult coworkers.

Office Friendships

At their best, office friendships promote goodwill among employees, improve communication, foster healthy competition, and generally make the office a better and more fun place to work. However, there can be a flip side: Sometimes office friendships breed backstabbing, gossip, hurt feelings, bad attitudes, aggressive competition, and sabotage.

Unlike friendships you form with schoolmates, neighbors, and other acquaintances, work friendships come with the caveat that something is always at stake—your career. You can—and should—develop healthy and fulfilling friendships with coworkers, just keep a few things in mind:

Remember what's at stake. If your pal at the gym or your old college roommate decides not to be your friend anymore, you may be sad, but when a work friendship goes bad, it can make your work life uncomfortable—or downright excruciating. Your former friend could tell other coworkers—or even a boss—unflattering things about you. You might even find yourself in competition for a prime assignment or promotion with your former friend, who will likely be less willing to play fair since your friendship went south.

Proceed with caution. You may think that your best friend at work is truly a best friend, and he or she might be. But research shows that it takes about three years for people to make fair judgments about whether someone is a true friend or not. So ask yourself: do you really know your coworker as well as you think you do?

Don't make the mistake of trusting someone with your career before you actually know them.

Establish boundaries. Work friends can have an influence on your career. It's best to establish boundaries for your office friendships that include what personal details you will reveal (does your office mate really need to know that you were almost arrested for streaking with your fraternity during college?), what subjects you will discuss, and what kinds of activities you will engage in together. The last thing you need is to reveal something embarrassing about yourself or say something mean about a coworker, then have it spread around the office after a friendship sours.

Be thoughtful. It's easy to create a circle of work friends that becomes a clique, which makes other coworkers feel left out. Avoid hurt feelings by including others as much as possible, by keeping inside jokes and information to a minimum, and by refusing to engage in hurtful gossip.

Think long term. You and your work friend might work in the same department and capacity now, but that might not always be so. Remember that you may one day be promoted and actually be your friend's manager, or vice versa. Conduct all of your work friendships in a way that will make such transitions as comfortable as possible.

Remember that appearances do count. It may not be fair, but people do make judgments about you based on appearances. If you are always going to lunch with the same coworker of the opposite sex, others might deduce that you are dating— even if your coworker is married. And if you strike up a close friendship with a superior, others might assume that your promotion was a result of your relationship. You don't have to be paranoid, but just keep in mind that people do talk— and try not to give them anything to talk about when it comes to you.

Diversify. Don't invest your entire emotional and social life in your work. Make sure that the friends you have at the office are just one part of your circle. That way, if office friendships expire, it won't be devastating. Plus, it will help you establish and maintain healthy boundaries with your office friends if you don't rely on them for everything.

Office romances

Office romances are common and you may find yourself attracted to one of your coworkers. However, remember that some organizations have a no-tolerance policy to discourage their employees from getting involved romantically. Even if it is accepted at your company, there are still some ground rules you should follow. To keep your career—and your heart—in one piece:

Follow the rules. Many companies have policies that outline what is and is not allowed when it comes to relationships between coworkers. Discreetly check on the rules before proceeding.

Keep it professional. Sure, you may be drunk with love, but nobody at work will want to hear about it. Keep in mind how your relationship may affect others at the office, and maintain professionalism at all times.

Keep it on even ground. Romantic relationships between managers and those they manage is strictly off limits, and usually prohibited by most companies. When the power balance is off in a relationship there's too much at stake, including careers and reputations. As the manager, you don't want to be accused of playing favorites with the one you love, or be accused of sexual harassment if the relationship sours. As the subordinate, you don't want your achievements to be seen as a result of your romantic relationship with the boss—it will destroy your credibility and breed contempt with coworkers.

Be discreet but not secretive. It's nearly impossible to keep a secret at the office, so don't even try. You'll appear to be dishonest or ashamed of your behavior and might incur more gossip. That said, you also don't have to scream your love from the mountaintop. It's probably best to disclose your relationship to management and to be honest should coworkers ask about it, but don't make your relationship the topic of every conversation.

Keep in touch with reality. Most dating relationships end in a break up. Try to conduct your relationship in a way that won't embarrass you or make you feel uncomfortable should it end. Remember: even if the relationship ends, your employment doesn't and you may have to work with your ex for years to come.

Difficult coworkers

Even though we hope that our coworkers will be friendly, helpful and fun, that's not always the case. From the simply annoying to the downright nasty, you will come across your share of difficult coworkers in the course of your career. You don't have to let these no-good coworkers bring you down. By recognizing some common personality types and learning how to deal with them, you can head off trouble and keep your career on track.

Chatty Cathy—or Charles: This coworker is well meaning but annoying, and is often a productivity killer. If the babble doesn't drive you crazy, the extra hours you'll spend making up for time lost while listening will.

- **What to do:** Try creating barriers that give the message that you're not available to chat—a closed door or wearing ear buds, for example—and try to head off talks by looking busy when you see this person coming your way (pick up the phone, or start typing like crazy). Don't encourage conversation—keep your answers to one word. And, if all else fails, have an honest but kind discussion—something along the lines of, "I really do like talking to you, but I find that I fall behind on my work when we talk too much. Let's try keeping our talks to a few minutes in the morning before work starts, or during our lunch break."

The Slacker: At one time or another, you will have someone in your department or on your team who is unable—or unwilling—to contribute in any meaningful way. This person might not have sufficient skills or education, may be disorganized or a procrastinator, could be insecure, or might just be lazy and willing to let someone else take up the slack. Whatever the reason, this coworker will likely make you work harder to make up for his or her shortcomings—and will make you mad in the process. This person might even take credit for your work when it's all said and done!

- **What to do:** Keep your nose to the grindstone. If you do your work and do it well, those in charge will realize where the fault lies. That said, don't try to make excuses for the slacker, and do everything you can to make him or her accountable for his or her actions and shortcomings. If the boss asks why a project missed deadline or didn't meet expectations, be honest but diplomatic.

The Gossiper: This coworker is trouble—and will stop at nothing to make him- or herself look better by discrediting others. He or she may seem friendly and fun at first, but only because he's trying to engage you in a conversation that he will mine for tidbits to use against you. Nothing is off limits with this coworker, from disclosing your personal information, to outright lying.

- **What to do:** Take the high road by refusing to engage in the gossiper's game. Don't give the gossiper anything to talk about; act professionally and prove his or her attacks wrong with your skills, dedication and performance. If you're a stellar employee, the gossiper won't have anything to say—and won't be believed even if he or she does.

Mr. or Ms. Toxic: A chronic complainer, if Mr. or Ms. Toxic is going to say anything, it's going to be negative. This is the coworker who immediately brings the mood of a room down.

- **What to do:** Don't let this person get to you, and don't let him or her get too far. Do what you can to cut him or her short, and try to counteract his or her negativity by being enthusiastic, complimentary and positive.

The Suck Up: Unfortunately, most offices have one of these. From spying on coworkers and reporting to the boss, to buying expensive holiday and birthday gifts for managers, this person will stop at nothing to gain a superior's attention and favor.

- **What to do:** Don't give the suck up any ammunition to take to the boss, but, mostly, ignore her or him. Most people can see a suck up coming for miles, and if you perform well, it will be noticed—despite the suck up's attempts to outdo you.

In general, when dealing with difficult coworkers:

- Accept that you and your coworkers are different and that you will have differences of opinion.

- Keep calm. Overt anger or frustration will only escalate the situation.

- Figure out what the source of the conflict is. Why do you find this person difficult? What bothers you about him/her?

- Keep it in perspective. Is your office mate's annoying habit of eating your food really worth possibly compromising your career?

- Create some solutions that you think will work.

- Discuss the situation with your coworker. In many cases, just talking about the problem may resolve it. Perhaps your coworker doesn't know she or he's being difficult—or maybe there are factors in play that you are unaware of that help explain her or his behavior.

- If you have tried but are unable to resolve problems with coworkers on your own, don't let it get out of control. Take your conflict to your manager or to human resources for some mediation.

Chapter 10

TEAMWORK

Little Leaguers and Navy SEALS, while miles apart in terms of age and experience, would probably have some very similar things to say about teamwork. Teamwork requires trust, for example. The individuals in a team have to respect each other and take personal responsibility. Each member of the team must exert maximum effort. The same rules apply whether you're playing baseball, protecting the free world, or managing a new software product: Individual success often depends on your ability to work well with others.

Today's work culture tends to minimize hierarchical structure and favors instead collaboration and team work. Companies generally recognize and reward employees who are creative, productive, responsible, and team players.

Being a team player comes easy for some people; for others it may be more difficult. Shyness, lack of confidence, an inability to surrender control or delegate, or an unwillingness to give up individual recognition to work for the greater good – all of these traits can impede successful teams.

But even if working on a team doesn't come naturally for you, you can develop your inner team player. Here's how:

What is a team?

A team is a collection of two or more people working interdependently toward a common goal and a shared reward. The part that should be emphasized, however, is working together. Anybody can throw a group of people together and tell them they have to get something done; a genuine team, however, works collaboratively to achieve better results than they would have attained individually. Members of successful teams are:

- Motivated by a common goal

- Able to overcome their need for individual recognition in order to work for the team's success

- Able to value diversity and capitalize on the strengths of fellow team members

- Focused on action rather than duty or a fear of failure

Teams that fail fall victim to inaction, poor communication, lack of leadership, or sense of common mission. In addition, egos, conflicting goals, and competition between members for recognition and rewards can destroy a team.

A true team, then, can be defined as a group of people who work together successfully and who have a common, well-understood purpose, specific goals, and a feeling of personal investment in the team's success—even above their own personal interest.

How a successful team works

Successful teams at work are not unlike successful sports teams. Think about what you know about championship teams. What do these teams have in common?

Clear expectations and consequences. To succeed, teams must fully understand what is expected of them, what outcomes they must produce, and the consequences of not achieving those goals.

Defined purpose. Team members should understand why a team has been formed and why they have been chosen to participate. They must also realize how the work of the team fits into the big picture of the organization's overall vision.

Strategy. Teams must have leadership, a framework for how work will be completed, a clear decision making and conflict resolution process, defined roles, and a system by which progress and success will be measured. In other words, teams must develop a strategy by which they will reach goals, complete work, and achieve success.

Communication, collaboration, and compromise. A team that works well knows how to communicate, work together, and compromise for the greater good.

Creativity and innovation. Teams understand that creative thinking, unique solutions, and new ideas are the foundation for success and they reward members for creativity and innovation. On a team, members understand that they can take reasonable risks and challenge the status quo.

Empowerment. In order to succeed, teams must feel that their work will be valued, that their success will have an impact on the company, and that they have the resources and authority necessary to achieve success.

Accountability. It's never one person's fault if a team fails—every team member has a responsibility for the results.

Overall culture that values teams. Teams that work well are part of companies that recognize the benefits of a team culture over that of a traditional, hierarchical organization. Companies that believe in team culture provide the resources, authority, and rewards necessary to build successful teams.

How to be a team player

Understanding the profile of a team player is the first step to being one. In general, a team player is:

Reliable. Team players can be counted on to meet deadlines, complete work that meets expectations, and follow through on commitments. Team players earn and maintain the trust of their teammates.

A good communicator. Team players are able to communicate ideas and opinions effectively. They are also good at listening—which is equally, if not more, important to good communication.

Eager to participate at all levels. A team player is an enthusiastic and willing participant in the work of the team and doesn't get hung up on whether work is "beneath them," outside of his/her job description, or someone else's responsibility. A true team player is willing to pitch in to do anything—from serving as a leader, to doing small administrative tasks.

Willing to share ideas, experience, and resources. A team player is invested in the success of the team and is willing to selflessly contribute—even if it means he or she might not receive individual recognition or reward.

Receptive and respectful of different ideas and perspectives. A team player understands that diversity is a strength, and exhibits respect and appreciation for other experiences, ideas, and points of view.

Cooperative and willing to compromise. Teams are built on the idea that "none of us are as strong as all of us." Team players understand that to fully capitalize on the strength of a team, cooperation and compromise are necessary.

Flexible. Not everything goes as planned. A team player understands that flexibility is necessary when it comes to accommodating the needs of others and in overcoming unanticipated circumstances and problems.

Responsible. Team players aren't finger pointers. They understand that being a member of a team means owning up to mistakes, taking fair share of the blame when failure occurs—and enjoying fair share of the rewards when the team succeeds.

A problem solver. A team player doesn't complain or worry about whose fault it is—he or she just solves the problem and gets the work done.

Respectful and supportive of team members. A team player genuinely cares about team members and gives them the respect, empathy, and support they need.

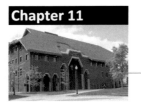

Chapter 11

MAKING CENT$ OF YOUR PAYCHECK

Sure, work should be fulfilling, challenging, and personally rewarding. But it's also really nice to get the paychecks. It's a pleasant surprise to open up your first "real" paycheck if you're working for the first time at a job that pays above minimum wage. It can also be a shock for another reason: deductions. From federal income and Social Security taxes to health insurance and flexible spending accounts, deductions from your paycheck add up faster than you can say "What the heck is FICA?" In the end, your paycheck may be just 50-60 percent of what you actually earned.

Whatever you do, don't ignore those strange abbreviations noted on your paycheck. Understanding where your money goes will not only make your smaller paycheck easier to swallow, but also protect you from potential accounting mistakes. In addition, by understanding where the funds from your paycheck are going, you can develop strategies to minimize deductions, from choosing the right number of allowances on your W-4 form to selecting the appropriate insurance plans for your needs.

Typical deductions

As mentioned before, there are various types of deductions that can reduce your take-home pay. Typical deductions from your paycheck include:

Federal income taxes

Federal income taxes take the heftiest chunk of cash from your paycheck. These funds go into a pot that pays for things that our elected leaders have deemed necessary, such as military to protect our country, social programs like food stamps and Medicare, and divisions of the government like the Department of Education, the Department of Agriculture, and the Department of Homeland Security.

The most confusing thing about Federal income taxes is the fact that different tax rates apply depending on your specific circumstances. This is because the Federal government uses a progressive tax system: taxable income levels are divided into brackets with lowest income brackets paying the least amount of tax. Tax brackets currently start at 10 percent and go to 35 percent. The more you earn, the more you pay.

So how does the progressive tax system work? Let's pretend for a moment that you were single in 2011 and you had a total income of $51,550. After adjustments, deductions, and credits, you had a taxable income of $42,458. Here's how your taxes would be figured if you were filing as a single taxpayer:

Applicable Tax Brackets on $42,458*	Tax Owed
10 percent tax on the first $8,500	$ 850
15 percent tax on the next $25,999	$ 3,900
25 percent tax on the last $7,959	$ 1,990
Total Tax Owed	**$6,740**

Current tax rate schedules are available online at www.irs.gov

Of course, adjustments, deductions and credits can significantly impact the amount of taxes you pay. For example, if you have children, make mortgage interest payments, or make contributions to charities, your tax bill will be lower. You have the ability to give the Federal government recommendations on how much money to take out of your paycheck through the W-4 form, a form you fill out on the first day you arrive at your new job. This form allows you to indicate the number of allowances you claim. Allowances are those factors that may lead you, at the end of the year, to pay less in taxes (like owning a home, having children, etc.).

In most cases, as a new graduate, you would probably claim one allowance on your W-4 form. Claiming zero will cause you to pay more in taxes and will probably result in a refund at the end of the year. Claiming two or higher will cause less taxes to be taken out of your monthly paycheck, but might mean you will owe taxes at the end of the year.

Keep in mind that receiving a big tax refund check from the government may not be such a good thing. That money, after all, was yours all along. Why let the government keep it all year, when you could use it or put it in an investment account and earn interest on it? Therefore, it's in your best interest to monitor your taxes year to year to determine the correct amount that should be deducted from your paycheck so that you avoid the big tax refund or, worse, a big tax bill. A tax professional can assist you with this decision.

State and local taxes

The Federal government isn't the only agency that needs your money to operate. Most (although not all) states, and some municipalities, also require citizens to pay income taxes to support their operations. Some use a progressive tax rate, similar in concept to the Federal government's, while others use a flat tax system where everyone pays the same percentage of their income, regardless of how much money they earn. To find out more about your local situation, contact your state and local government offices or consult with a local accountant.

Social Security and Medicare taxes

As a United States citizen, you are required pay social security and Medicare taxes on your wages – commonly referred to as FICA (Federal Insurance Contributions Act). These taxes are used to fund retirement income and health insurance to citizens 65 and over. Currently, every worker is required to contribute 12.4 percent of his/her annual income to social security and an additional 2.9 percent to Medicare. In most cases, you pay half of this tax and your employer is required to pay the other half. However, if you are self-employed, you are required to pay the entire amount (commonly referred to as the Self-Employment Tax).

Insurance deductions

Many companies provide employees reduced cost insurance as a benefit of employment. This can include health, dental, vision, disability, and supplemental insurance. To receive this benefit, you agree to pay a portion of the insurance expense, usually 50 percent. Therefore, if your insurance plan costs $4,680.00 per year and your employer agrees to pay half, the rest will be deducted from your paycheck. If you are paid on a weekly basis, it will be deducted over 52 weeks, so $45.00 will be deducted from each of your paychecks.

In some cases, your employer may offer you a variety of reduced cost insurance programs. These are described in more detail in the next chapter. If you are fortunate enough to receive reduced cost insurance options from your employer, you should seriously consider taking advantage of these options, as insurance can be very expensive. Of course, always be sure to weigh the benefits of each plan and select the program that fits your needs.

Other deductions

There are a variety of other deductions that could affect your paycheck. Some companies charge for parking, which is then deducted from paychecks. Some companies offer flexible spending accounts for medical purposes or child care expenses, in which case funds are deducted from your paycheck without being taxed by the government, then deposited into an account and reimbursed to you as you provide receipts of medical bills and/or child care costs. Because you don't pay taxes on this money, it saves you money. Your company may ask employees to donate to fundraising campaigns for organizations such as United Way or Red Cross, and, if you choose to participate, your donation is deducted from your paycheck.

Reviewing your paycheck

Review every pay stub you receive to ensure that you understand all the deductions. If you do not understand what a deduction is for, or how the amount of a specific deduction was determined, contact your payroll department. Remember, it's your money—you should know where it is going. After you review your paycheck, file it so that you'll be able to reference it easily or access it if you decide to take a loan out for a major purchase.

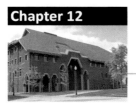

Chapter 12

UNDERSTANDING EMPLOYEE BENEFITS

Vacation time. Retirement contributions. The ability to bring your dog to work. When evaluating the value of your job, your salary is really only half of the picture. In fact, the other half of the picture – your benefits – can be just as important to your quality of life as the amount of money you make.

Most full-time employees receive some form of health insurance programs, retirement plans, and paid leave. Some companies even offer free or reduced cost childcare, free gym memberships, paid leave for new parents, access to free or reduced cost education, and flexible work hours. However, in this age of rising insurance costs and shrinking profits, it is becoming more difficult for employers to offer all the benefits they would like. In fact, many companies are struggling to even offer health insurance coverage.

In this chapter, we'll discuss the most common types of benefits you might receive as a full-time employee, from paid time off to flexible working conditions.

Sure bet benefits

There are certain benefits employers are required by law to provide. These include:

- Providing time off to vote, serve on a jury, and perform military service.
- Complying with all workers' compensation requirements.
- Withholding FICA taxes from employees' paychecks, as well as paying the employer's portion of FICA taxes.
- Paying state and federal unemployment taxes, thus providing benefits for unemployed workers.
- Contributing to state short-term disability programs in states where such programs exist.
- Complying with the Federal Family and Medical Leave (FMLA).

Any benefits provided above and beyond these are completely at the discretion of the employer, but chances are your employer will offer at least a small menu of benefits to you. Some benefits, such as paid vacation, come at no cost to you, while others, such as health insurance, may be subsidized by your employer but may also require you to pay a portion of the cost as well, should you choose to enroll.

At the start of your employment, you should carefully consider all of the benefits offered by your employer, making sure that you understand each one and how it can impact you. It's okay not to take advantage of benefits you feel are of no use to you—free child care, for example, if you don't have children—but remember that ignoring certain benefits—like retirement plans in which your employer matches your contributions—is like throwing money away. Below are descriptions of several of the more common types of employee benefits.

Vacation and sick leave

Your employer will almost certainly offer you some form of vacation and sick leave. To begin with, you will most likely receive a few paid holidays a year, such as Christmas Day, Thanksgiving Day, Fourth of July, and maybe a few others.

Depending on your employer, you may also receive paid vacation time, although at the start of your career you probably won't have much. At most companies, the amount of vacation time an employee receives depends on the length of time the employee has worked at the company. For example, employees with one year of service may receive one week of paid vacation, while an employee with 10 years of service may receive three weeks.

U.S. employers also, according to the Department of Labor, offer an average of nine paid sick days to employees. These are days that can be used during an illness or for scheduled doctor appointments.

Many companies use a "Paid Time Off" system for paid leave, in which employees accrue days off over time that can be used for any purpose the employee chooses. For example, in a Paid Time Off system, employees might earn 8 hours (or one work day) per pay period of paid time off. If there are 26 pay periods per year, an employee earns 208 hours per year, or 26 days of paid time off to be used as the employee chooses – for vacation, sick time, or other reasons.

Some companies will reimburse employees periodically for a portion of paid time off that they don't use; check with your human resources department about this option so you don't lose out if you accidentally miss a deadline.

Health insurance

In this age of exorbitant medical costs, health insurance is what most employees name as the most important benefit provided by an employer. Health insurance offers medical benefits covering most of the care doctors and nurses provide. Sometimes health insurance also includes dental and vision coverage, usually at a small additional cost. These programs may also provide health care support to an employee's children or other dependents. Some plans allow the employee to have health insurance even after he/she retires. Common types of health insurance plans include:

Health Maintenance Organizations (HMOs)

HMOs are groups of physicians and other health professionals who have agreed to offer their services for a fixed fee, paid by the insurance program and the patient, usually in the form of a co-pay of as little as $10.00. HMOs are generally less expensive than other options, but restrict your choice of health care providers to those participating in the plan. If you choose to see a provider not participating in the plan, the cost of your care is not reimbursed. HMOs also require referrals for care beyond your primary care physician and may have more stringent limits on the kinds of care you can receive.

Preferred Provider Organizations (PPOs)
As with an HMO system, PPOs have a list of medical service providers, commonly referred to as "preferred providers." You are encouraged to choose a provider on this list, but you also have the option of choosing a provider that is not on the list. Participants are reimbursed at a lower level when they visit out-of-network providers. These plans are usually more expensive than HMOs, but offer more flexibility in the care you receive and may not require referrals.

Fee-For-Service Program
Although not as common as the previously mentioned health care options, the fee-for-service program allows participants to choose their own medical provider. Participants are then reimbursed for medical care services. Oftentimes, a participant pays a set amount, known as a deductible, before he or she is reimbursed for medical costs. There may be other plan requirements including shared payments for medical services and prescription. There may also be a maximum amount of medical costs the plan will cover in a lifetime.

If your employer offers health insurance, you should enroll. Although you may be young and healthy, illness, health conditions and accidents can happen at any time, and one extended illness, injury, or hospital stay can cost tens of thousands of dollars – putting you in debt for years to come. That being said, you don't necessarily have to enroll in the most expensive option available. Weigh your options carefully and choose the insurance program that fits your needs, but don't pay for additional services and benefits that you don't need.

Disability insurance
Disability insurance provides financial support when an employee becomes injured or ill and is unable to do his/her job. The two types of disability insurance are short-term and long-term.

Short-Term Disability Insurance
Short-term disability coverage often begins right away if an employee is in an accident, or it may begin within a few weeks of an illness or some other disability. For example, this coverage would provide a portion of the employee's salary to someone hurt in a car accident who needs a few weeks off from work to recover. In addition, some short-term disability policies cover time away from work for pregnancy and the weeks after giving birth.

Long-Term Disability Insurance
Long-term disability coverage is offered by employers less commonly than short-term disability insurance. This type of insurance provides benefits to an employee when a long-term or permanent illness, injury, or disability makes it

impossible for the employee to continue to perform his/her job duties. Long-term disability benefits often last until retirement age.

Some states also offer disability insurance and require employers operating in that state to enroll employees in the programs. If this is not the case in your state, you should still consider enrolling in disability insurance, even if it is at an added expense to you. Though it may be unlikely, a short period of disability can cost you your financial security for years to come. The added expense of purchasing disability insurance through your employer is usually minimal – and can save you a lot of money and stress in the future should you encounter a situation where you are unable to work because of a disability.

Life insurance

Your employer may also offer free or low-cost life insurance plans. The main purpose of life insurance is to provide financial support to an employee's family in case of death. The beneficiary of a life insurance plan is usually a relative such as a parent, spouse, or child. Life insurance pays a lump sum benefit to the beneficiary of the policy after an employee's death. If you are not currently providing support to any dependents such as a spouse, child, or elderly or dependent parent, you may find it unnecessary to enroll in your employer's life insurance plan, especially if it is at an additional cost to you. However, if you have dependents, life insurance is always a good idea.

Retirement programs

Retirement plans are savings and/or investment plans designed to develop a fund to be used to provide you money to live on in the years following your retirement. Although your retirement years may seem a long way off, don't ignore the value of starting early when it comes to planning for this time in your life. Not convinced? Consider the following example:

A Recent Graduate . . .	A Not So Recent Graduate . . .
• Begins investing for retirement at age 21.	• Begins investing for retirement at age 30.
• Invests $2,000 each year until age 29 and does NOT invest any more money in retirement after that.	• Invests $2,000 each year and continues to do so until age 65.
• Total contributions: $18,000 at at a 10 percent compounding rate of return.	• Total contributions: $70,000 at a 10 percent compounding rate of return.
• Value at age 65: **$839,556**	• Value at age 65: **$598,253**

The bottom line: If your employer offers a retirement program, take advantage of it!

Typically, retirement plans offered by employers are contribution plans. This means that participants make contributions to individual investment accounts;

the resulting benefits are based on the contributions plus their earned interest. Depending on the kind of plan offered by your company, your employer will contribute to your plan or you will have to contribute your own money to the fund, which may or may not be matched by your employer. The most common forms of retirement programs include:

401(k), 403(b) or 457 Plans
The names of these plans refer to the section numbers of the Internal Revenue Code that authorizes them. The primary difference between these plans is who can offer them. For example, private companies offer the 401(k) plan, whereas the 403(b) and 457 plans are offered by non-profit, tax-exempt organizations. Regardless of the type of organization you work for, the plans are very similar. Your employer selects different investment options for you to choose from. Usually, the investment options vary in terms of risk and aggressiveness. With these plans, you will contribute your own money to the fund, which may or may not be matched by your employer. One benefit of these plans is that they are portable, meaning that you can take the money with you should you decide to change employers.

Profit Sharing Plan
With a profit-sharing employee retirement plan, your employer makes contributions that may vary from year to year based on the company's profitability. If your employer makes contributions to a profit-sharing retirement plan, these contributions and earnings accumulate tax-free until you withdraw them. This type of plan cannot be transferred and applied to the retirement plan at your new employer, but can be transferred to your own personal retirement account.

Employee Pension Plans
In the past, pension plans sponsored by employers or labor unions were typically "defined benefits plans" in which a specific dollar amount for each year of service to a company was provided each month to the employee upon retirement, regardless of contributions. For example, a company might provide $100 per year of service. An employee with 30 years of service would then receive $3,000 per month upon retirement. Like the profit sharing plan, these plans are not portable – meaning that when you leave the company, you cannot take your accumulated benefits and apply it to the retirement plan at your new employer. However, you can set up your own personal retirement account to have the funds transferred to.

Educational assistance
Educational assistance programs usually provide full or partial reimbursement of employee expenses for books, tuition, and fees associated with advancing or maintaining their level of education. Most likely, your employer will require that the education support your current position or another position at the company (an accounting firm, for example, will pay for employees to earn their CPA, but won't pay for an employee to attend nursing school), and may require that you attend specific schools.

Transportation subsidies

Many companies, especially those located in cities, offer employees assistance with transportation by providing free or reduced cost bus or train passes, shuttle services, or carpool assistance services. They may also offer free or reduced-cost parking. Often, cities or states will provide incentives to companies to do so in an effort to reduce traffic or emissions. If your company offers transportation benefits, you may be able to commute to work for free on your city's subway system, receive free shuttle service from the bus station to the front door of your office, or be matched with coworkers who live near you and would be willing to share a ride to work.

Alternative work schedules

More and more companies are offering alternative work schedules to meet their own and their employees' needs. Alternative work schedules allow employees to work outside of the traditional 9 to 5, five days a week work schedule. Employers, as well, may like alternative work schedules and arrangements because they can reduce overhead (fewer employees in house, fewer desks needed, less electricity used), increase coverage (employees working odd hours are there to answer the phones), and increase productivity (fewer missed days because employees are happy and able to attend to their lives outside of work). Some common alternative work arrangements include:

Flextime

Flextime gives employees the flexibility of choosing the hours they will work, within the limits set by their employer. For example, an employee taking advantage of flextime might work four ten-hour days instead of five eight-hour ones, and take Fridays off. Or an employee who needs to be home early to care for children coming home from school might choose to work from 7 a.m. to 3 p.m. instead of the typical 9 to 5 work day. Flextime is great for employees who have special circumstances (like children or a second job), or who just like the flexibility of working when they want.

Telecommuting

Telecommuting is working from home or another auxiliary space, using the Internet, email, phone, and fax to communicate with the office. While not all work circumstances make telecommuting possible (a nurse, for example, can't provide care from home), those positions where an in-person presence is not necessary are becoming increasingly more off-site positions. Even those who don't telecommute on a regular basis may occasionally take advantage of telecommuting – on days when a child is home sick or on a day when they must be at home to let a plumber in but don't want to miss a day of work. While it sounds attractive, telecommuting does come with its own set of pros and cons, and isn't for everyone. Many telecommuters cite lack of human interaction as a downside of working from home, while others lack the self-motivation to get their work done without the structure of an office. If your employer offers telecommuting, consider very carefully whether you have the personality to be a productive telecommuter.

Job sharing

A job share is when two people fulfill the requirements of one job by dividing the work week and work functions between them. This arrangement is perfect for working parents, people who are completing an educational degree, or those who have other jobs, hobbies, or circumstances that make working a 40-hour week difficult. Job sharing does, however, require a good partnership and good communication between the job sharers.

Other benefits

Every company has its own menu of benefits. Some are more extensive than others, but don't count out the small benefits your company may offer. Things like free health screenings and flu shots, reduced-cost gym memberships, free educational seminars on both work subjects (i.e. an "Effective Management" seminar) or non-work subjects (i.e. a "File You Own Taxes" class), or reduced cost services at local vendors like dry cleaners, restaurants, or travel agencies are commonly provided by employers – and can add up to hundreds or even thousands of dollars in savings over the course of a year. Check out what your employer offers!

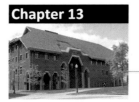

Chapter 13

EMPLOYEE RIGHTS

Many organizations greet new employees with a handbook of rules, policies, and expectations. As a new employee, you'll learn about dress codes, for example, as well as what's considered appropriate use of technology. There's a lot to learn about their expectations of you—but you should also know that there are rules, policies, and standards that they have to follow, too.

The Federal government and your state government both have laws designed to protect the rights of workers. Your organization will likely also have policies, rules, and protocols in place to help reinforce existing laws and to help create a positive and productive work environment. Even if your organization doesn't have a written policy regarding discrimination, harassment, or unemployment, it must still follow federal and state laws that provide these kinds of protections for workers. This chapter will provide you with an overview of your rights as an employee as well as an in-depth look at specific rights, such as maternity/paternity leave and discrimination protection.

Overview of employee rights

As an employee, you are entitled to the following rights:

Discrimination protection: It is against the law to discriminate during hiring and firing or while considering job performance, salary, or promotions on the basis of age, gender, race, disability, medical condition, national origin, religion or creed. Some states also protect you from being discriminated against on the basis of sexual orientation or even your weight.

Harassment protection: You are generally protected from being harassed verbally, physically, or sexually while on the job.

Safe work environment: Employers must provide a safe working environment for employees and must provide compensation insurance to cover medical and disability costs should an employee be injured or become ill due to something that occurred on the job.

Unemployment insurance: Employers must pay for unemployment insurance to cover unemployment benefits to workers who are fired or laid off.

Wage protection: There are laws and protections in place to ensure that workers receive a minimum wage and fair wages for overtime work.

Job protection: In most cases, your job is protected should you need to take leave to attend to jury duty; fulfill military service; adopt or give birth to a child;

receive treatment or recover from an extended illness; or care for a sick child or parent.

Breaks: While no federal law requires employers to offer breaks to employees, many states require that employers make bathroom facilities available, and allow employees to take time to use bathroom facilities, eat, and rest from duties.

Whistleblower protection: You are protected by law from being fired for reporting your employer for breaking laws (or "blowing the whistle").

Personal information protection: Your employer is only allowed to obtain and judge certain information about you. This information includes credit history, criminal record, medical information, prior salary, and personal information such as your marital or parental status, age, or religious or philosophical beliefs. For example, a potential employer can ask if you have ever been convicted of a felony, but cannot ask if you plan on having children.

The specifics of these rights are quite extensive and may differ from state to state and industry to industry, so spend some time familiarizing yourself with the laws, standards, and regulations that apply to your position and the industry you will be working in. The following sections also highlight a few of the common questions and concerns regarding employee rights.

If you get sick

At some point, most people require leave from their job due to illness. Some people may even experience a work-related illness or injury.

The bad news is that there is no federal law requiring your employer to give you paid sick time or unpaid leave unless you have a disability or are covered by FMLA, the Federal Family and Medical Leave Act. The good news is that most employers provide employees with sick time to give them time to recover from illnesses or injuries. Depending on the organization, the number of sick days allowed varies, as do other related requirements and restrictions. For example, you may be required to furnish a doctor's note to prove your illness, you may lose your sick days if you don't use them within a certain amount of time, or you may only be able to save up a certain amount of sick days to use at a later time. Be sure to familiarize yourself with the details and specifics of your organization's sick leave policy.

If your benefits package comes with sick days, your employer should not stop you from using them or threaten you with punishment or termination if you use them legitimately and follow organization policy. If your benefits package does not include sick days, you can legally be punished or terminated for abusing your company's sick policy or for taking a sick day. However, your organization can not fire you if your illness or injury falls under FMLA or disability laws, even if sick time is not part of your benefits package.

FMLA provides American workers the right to take up to 12 weeks of unpaid leave per year to attend to serious medical conditions. You must have worked for your employer for at least one year, your employer is entitled to a doctor's certification that your medical leave is necessary, and, if possible, you must give at least thirty days' notice of your intent to take leave (this may not always be possible in the case of medical emergencies). Leave does not have to be taken all at once (you may, for example, take a few days per month for chemotherapy treatments). FMLA leave can also be taken to care for a sick child or parent.

While your employer is not required to pay you during your leave as part of FMLA, your job will be protected and you cannot be terminated during your leave. If your employer employs fewer than 50 people, however, it is not required to adhere to FMLA standards.

If you are injured or become ill due to the circumstances of your job, you most likely are eligible for workers' compensation insurance. Workers' compensation insurance—often called workmans' comp.—will generally cover all of your medical expenses, wages lost while you are sick or injured, and any job retraining or training that you might need to prepare you for your return to work or to help you change positions should your injury or illness render you unable to return to your prior position. Usually you will receive about two-thirds of your normal salary while on workers' compensation, but because this compensation is not subject to taxes, it will probably be about equal to what your paycheck is after taxes.

Your organization maintains a workers' compensation insurance policy that covers all of these costs. At the start of your employment, you should familiarize yourself with your company's policies and coverage. Review what you would need to do and what things you would need to document should you be injured or become ill, and how much coverage you would receive. That way, if you are injured or get ill, you will know what to do and will have less to worry about at an already stressful time.

Maternity/paternity leave

Whether planned or unplanned, a pregnancy should not interfere with your current employment or career status.

Maternity and/or paternity leave is the time a mother or father takes off from work at the birth or adoption of a child. Unfortunately, paid maternity or paternity leave is not commonly offered by U.S. employers, though that is changing as more and more progressive companies realize the benefit of offering this kind of leave to their employees. Employers who offer paid maternity and paternity leave often find that they are able to attract and retain high quality employees by offering this benefit, and that they enjoy more productivity and loyalty from employees who have been given adequate time to care for a new child before returning to work.

Even if your employer does not offer paid maternity or paternity leave, you can still take time off to care for a new child without losing your job. FMLA, as described earlier in this chapter, gives employees up to 12 weeks of unpaid leave to care for a new child. You also can use a combination of your employer-provided sick time, short-term disability, and vacation time, all of which will be paid, as well as unpaid leave to cover the amount of time you would like to take off to care for your new child. Every employer has different rules regarding what kind of leave and how much leave you can apply to maternity or paternity leave.

Sexual harassment

Sexual harassment is defined as the unwelcome sexual conduct of a supervisor, colleague, or client. This sexual conduct could include sexual comments, pressure for sexual favors, unwelcome touching, sexual jokes, the display of degrading sexual material or even sexual assault. Anybody can be sexually harassed – male or female, young or old. However, to be truly illegal, behavior must fall under the two definitions of sexual harassment that are recognized by the courts:

Quid Pro Quo Sexual Harassment

In this kind of sexual harassment, an employee is discriminated against, denied promotions or raises, or is subject to other consequences because he or she refuses the sexual demands of a supervisor or colleague. For example, if your boss asks you on a date but you decline and are then demoted as a result, this may be quid pro quo sexual harassment.

Hostile Work Environment Harassment

In this kind of sexual harassment, unwelcome sexual conduct in your work place is so pervasive that it negatively affects your work environment and causes your work to suffer, even if you are not a direct subject of the sexual conduct. For example, if two coworkers are constantly telling sexual jokes for all the office to hear and the boss does nothing, despite the conduct being brought to his or her attention, this might be hostile work environment harassment.

While conduct that falls under the definitions of quid pro quo or hostile work environment harassment is the easiest to legally prove as illegal sexual harassment, the U.S. Supreme Court stated in a 1998 ruling that any sexual conduct that a "reasonable person" could determine was causing discrimination in the workplace could be defined as sexual harassment. In other words, even though behavior may not be explicitly quid pro quo or hostile work environment, you may still be able to prove in a court that the behavior was sexual harassment.

To curb sexual harassment and to avoid legal ramifications, many organizations have implemented strict policies regarding sexual conduct at the office. For example, to discourage any appearances of impropriety, your company may make sexual relations between employees a behavior that is punishable by termination, or it may have strong consequences for employees who tell jokes or stories of a sexual nature. Many companies also have training programs in place to teach employees what sexual harassment is and how and why it should be avoided. You should make sure that you understand your company's policies regarding sexual harassment – so you can understand when a supervisor's or coworker's behavior has crossed the line, and so you can be sure that your behavior doesn't. If you believe that you may be a victim of sexual harassment:

- Keep a record of occurrences, including any messages or emails that can document the behavior.

- Make your harasser aware of his or her behavior and ask him/her to stop. Even better, write a letter demanding that the harassment stop and keep a copy.

- Obtain a copy of your company's sexual harassment policy and reporting system so that you can follow your company's procedures.

- Take your complaint to a superior or to your human resources department, if applicable.

- If reporting the harassment to your employer does not stop the harassment, look into reporting the harassment to the proper government or law enforcement agency, or hiring an attorney.

Sexism, racism, favoritism

Maybe you suspect that your boss doesn't like you. Maybe he or she gives other employees better assignments, pays them more, or promotes them above you – even though, in your opinion, you deserve it more. Is this discrimination? Maybe. Is it illegal? Maybe not.

If your boss simply likes another employee better than you and acts accordingly, this is not illegal discrimination, it is simply favoritism. No matter how unfair or unethical it may seem, it's not against the law for a supervisor to like one employee more than another, to find certain employees annoying and treat them accordingly, or to think one employee is more qualified than another because he or she shares the same alma mater as the boss.

If you suspect a supervisor is playing favorites, you can take it to human resources, but they don't necessarily have to do anything about it. On the other hand, many organizations have policies discouraging this kind of behavior, and may have systems in place to ensure that employees are not victims of favoritism.

For discrimination to be illegal, an employer must negatively single out employees or potential employees on the basis of their protected class, which includes race, color, religion, creed, sex, national origin, age (older than 40), disability, veteran status, and sometimes (depending on state law) sexual orientation, marital or parental status, or weight. Legally, employers cannot discriminate on the basis of the above reasons in any aspect of employment, including:

- Hiring and firing
- Compensation, assignment, or classification of employees
- Transfer, promotion, layoff, or recall

- Job advertisements
- Recruitment
- Testing
- Use of company facilities
- Training and apprenticeship programs
- Fringe benefits
- Pay, retirement plans, and disability leave

If you suspect that you are the victim of illegal discrimination, ask yourself the following questions:

1. Are you a member of a protected class?
2. Were you fully qualified for your position? In other words, were there any other legitimate reasons for the adverse action taken against you?
3. Was a negative action taken against you? For example, were you fired?
4. Were you treated differently than an equally qualified person who isn't in your protected class?
5. Did managers or supervisors regularly make rude or derogatory comments related to work and directed at members of your protected class? For example, "Women don't make good engineers."
6. Is there a history of discrimination at your company?
7. Is there a noticeable lack of diversity at your company?
8. Have you noticed that other employees in protected classes are singled out for negative treatment?
9. Are there statistics that show favoritism toward or bias against any group at your company (for example, 99 percent of managers are male)?
10. Did your employer violate well-established company policy in the way it treated you?
11. Did your company hire or promote less-qualified, non-protected employees in the same job?

If the answer is yes to several of these questions, you may be a victim of discrimination.

Your first step should be to exhaust your options within your organization. If you believe your supervisor or another superior is discriminating against you, your company may have policies and systems in place to handle your grievance fairly. Familiarize yourself with the discrimination policies at your organization (which should be outlined in your employee handbook or on your organization's Web site), then see your human resources department or representative to discuss the issue or make a formal complaint. Depending on how your organization handles discrimination complaints, you may be removed from the chain of command of the accused supervisor or department, asked to document your complaints so that action can be taken against the accused, or be asked to participate in mediation.

If you feel that you did not receive adequate or fair treatment from your employer or if you believe that your entire company is guilty of discrimination, you can go further. You can hire an attorney to advise you of your rights and the merit of your case, and to represent you in legal actions against your company. If you don't want to or are unable to hire an attorney, both Federal and state governments have agencies designed to investigate discrimination claims against employers.

The Equal Employment Opportunity Commission (EEOC), headquartered in Washington, D.C., is the federal agency responsible for investigating discrimination claims against employers. EEOC district and area offices are located throughout the country and you can find one in your area by checking your phone book or Internet listings. However, if your employer is small, with fewer than 15 employees, your rights are not protected by the EEOC. Instead, you should contact your state's fair employment practice agency, which you also can find in your phone book or Internet listings.

Jury and military duty

Most states have laws requiring employers to give workers unpaid leave to attend to civic duties like voting, jury duty, and military service. Some states even require that this leave be paid by the employer.

Whether or not the law requires it, the Bureau of Labor Statistics reports that 87 percent of all employers do pay employees for time missed to attend to jury duty. You should familiarize yourself with your state's laws regarding jury duty, as well as your employer's policies about leave needed for jury duty. Generally, you cannot be penalized or terminated for missing work to serve on a jury. If your employer threatens to take action against you because you have missed work due to jury duty, you probably have the legal right to challenge this.

As with jury duty, if you are called to serve in the military, most states require your employer to provide you unpaid leave and re-employ you without any loss of benefits, reduction in status or pay, once your service is completed. This includes situations where you are drafted, are called to service as part of a National Guard or reserve unit, or must complete regular training as part of your military duties.

Each state has its own specific conditions and requirements concerning lawful leave for military duty, and individual employers also may have additional requirements or even benefits regarding employees who must take a leave of absence to serve in the military (for example, they may pay you for the first 90 days). If there is a possibility that you may be called to serve your country, you should make sure that you understand your state's laws and your employer's policies regarding military leave.

Job descriptions and office protocol

As a new and inexperienced employee, you are probably eager to prove your abilities and reluctant to say no to any task your supervisor assigns you. But you should know that, while being agreeable and a team player will definitely work in your favor, being walked all over is not a requirement. So how do you know when what your boss is asking of you has crossed the line? And how do you say no and still save face?

Most companies would frown on supervisors using company resources (namely you) for personal gain. You have been hired and are being paid to perform functions and complete work that benefits your company and fulfills its mission —not to address your boss's holiday cards or pick his or her kids up from soccer practice. In some cases—if you work for the government or some other publicly funded body, for example—it may even be considered an illegal misuse of public resources.

That said, depending on your job function, there are sometimes legitimate reasons for doing things outside of your job description that personally benefit your boss. If, for example, your boss is on deadline to complete an important report that everyone in your department has contributed to, and she or he asks you if you can pick lunch up, you'd be pitching in for the good of the company by getting her or him a sandwich. You'd also likely be considered a colossal jerk for telling your boss it's "not in your job description." On the other hand, if your boss sees you as nothing more than a personal gopher and you find yourself spending more time on his or her personal matters than on the responsibilities for which you were hired, he or she's most likely abusing power, breaking corporate policies, and taking advantage of your inexperience. Your boss's requests are probably crossing the line if:

- The duties are performed on your own time, with no compensation.

- Your supervisor asks you not to tell anyone else about the chore.

- You end up working extra hours to complete your own work because you've spent so much time on personal favors for your boss.

- You find yourself having to explain to others how you are spending your time and why you are performing the tasks that you are.

- You are ever asked to do something unethical, illegal, or in violation of other employees' rights or privacy.

If you find that your boss is taking advantage of you, the best tactic is to explain clearly but diplomatically that, while you are happy to help out, these extra jobs are taking you away from the primary responsibilities for which you were hired. If that doesn't work, you may have to discuss your complaints with someone higher up on the chain of command, or with someone in the human resources department.

Remember that as an entry-level employee you may not always be given the most desirable tasks. You will probably become well-acquainted with the copy machine, the fax machine, the filing cabinets, and the phone system during the early years of your career. You may even be asked to make the coffee or go pick up lunch. That's okay – this is a time to prove yourself and create a place for yourself at your company. But, you also have a right to be treated fairly and your company likely has policies in place to make sure that you are.

Workplace abuse

While physical violence and abuse is rare, research indicates that one in five workers is a victim of emotional and verbal abuse. Some experts estimate that the cost of workplace abuse is high—nearly $200 million in lost productivity, health consequences, employee turnover, and general workplace dysfunction.

By some accounts, workplace abuse has increased in recent years due to the stresses of modern life, including dual income families, longer work weeks, added duties and fewer workers, commuting ills, and so on. As a result, more and more companies are putting policies in place to define workplace abuse and establish clear ways to curb it. Your company likely has an employee handbook that outlines which behaviors are acceptable and which are not, as well as the potential consequences of engaging in unacceptable—or abusive—behavior.

Most states do not have specific laws regarding abuse in the workplace; however, the same laws that protect you in your home and in public are also in play in the work place. If a colleague or supervisor behaves in a way that would be defined as illegal in the world at large, then what they are doing is abusive and should be reported to those in charge at your company, and possibly to authorities as well.

Even if the bad behavior of a boss or coworker is not defined as illegal, your company may have policies in place that prohibit it. For example, calling someone stupid or cursing at them isn't necessarily illegal or punishable by law, but your company may not allow your boss to do these things without repercussions.

Don't think that because you are new, inexperienced, or young that you have to put up with bad behavior, insults or threats. Even if the person abusing you is your superior or boss, you do have recourse. Familiarize yourself with your company's policies regarding employee behavior and the systems in place for reporting abuse. It can also be useful to keep a record of abusive behavior as it occurs so that you can document a pattern of abuse.

And, of course, if at any time you feel physically threatened or in danger of any kind, remove yourself from the situation immediately and report it to both your employer and the authorities.

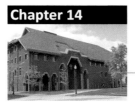

Chapter 14

GO BEYOND AVERAGE

Average. Even the word is boring. Kind of nasally and slow, like a whine. It's no surprise, then, that no one wants to be average. We want below average cholesterol and above average intelligence, but even that seems a little dull. Who wants to go to a restaurant or a doctor with just an "above average" reputation? Who wants to be labeled "above average"? Bleh. It's as good as saying "not excellent."

So let's get rid of that word right here. In your work life you want to be way beyond average. Not even in the same realm. Instead, you'll be excellent. Superior. Remarkable. Now, in school a person needs simply to meet the standard in order to pass the class. But in work if you just meet the standard you could end up with job paralysis. Instead, you want to advance your knowledge and experience (and, yes, your salary) so you need to go beyond the basic job description on a regular basis. A dynamic, fulfilling career is made up of many daily decisions to exceed expectations.

Starting your job with the mission of proving to both your supervisors and yourself that you've got the right stuff will instill a habit of excellence. You'll become so accustomed to welcoming challenges and doing your best that remarkable job performance will be your norm. And you'll find that the energy you give will come back to you.

Now, the advice in this chapter is common sense, the stuff of Abe Lincoln stories and more than one commencement address. But there's a reason these tips are repeated in various forms by successful people: Going beyond expectations is what separates the average and above average professional from the remarkable one.

Work a full day

We know, we know. This one seems painfully obvious. However, even though conventional wisdom says to work a full day at your job if you want to excel, managers still report that many employees arrive a little late and leave a little early. And take a lot of breaks. Now, circadian rhythm and psychological studies may show that flexible hours plus a nap in the middle of the day boosts productivity and efficiency, but let's just say that most of the working world hasn't caught up to this way of thinking.

People notice if you arrive late and leave early, and they really, really notice if you show up for a meeting with sleep creases on your face. No matter how much you're actually getting done, timeliness can't be underestimated. If you get to the office early and leave a little late, you'll establish yourself as someone who is committed and hardworking. And that's the kind of getting noticed you want.

Do your job well

Whatever you're doing, take pride in your work. Two sayings come to mind here: "All work is meaningful" and "Way leads on to way." And while these might sound pat when you're doing double data entry and extreme filing, they're cliché because they're true. We all start somewhere, and if it's in document shredding, well, be a fast, thorough (and ethical!) shredder. Write a book about it—*Zen and the Art of Document Shredding*—or a comedy routine. Or come up with a better method of shredding and patent it. Or simply finish the shredding early and volunteer to take on a task that will really challenge you and showcase your talents.

Consider This ...

Treat Every Project Like a Raise Depends on It

Every day, and with every task, ask yourself if you're working to your full potential. Sure, you're past tryouts (the interviews and probationary period) and have "made the team," but you still need to prove your worth to the organization on a daily basis. This will benefit you and the organization you work for. People who treat every task and project like a raise depends on it tend to have a higher rate of job satisfaction and fulfillment. And they are more likely to earn rewards like promotions and raises.

Take the initiative

One great way to demonstrate your willingness to work hard is to take the initiative and volunteer for projects, committees, and additional training. These volunteer efforts could mean taking on gigantic projects—rewriting a computer program, for instance, or creating a style manual—or even offering assistance with the little tasks that aren't glamorous but simply need to get done, like binding a report or running copies.

Taking on tasks outside your job requirements, whether those tasks are challenging or basic, will help you learn more about the organization, develop your skills, and establish strong relationships with your supervisors and colleagues.

Make the most of your mistakes

Superior job performance includes dealing with mistakes in a constructive way. The below average employee covers up or blows off mistakes; the average employee minimizes his or her mistakes by passing or maybe "sharing" the buck; the excellent employee takes responsibility for his or her mistakes, learns from them, and moves on. It's not a question if you'll make mistakes but how you'll deal with them when you do. If you're up front about an error, reflect on it, and self-correct, the mistake itself won't be nearly as memorable as the lasting impression of your integrity and dedication to doing your job right.

Contribute positively to the organization

All employees contribute to the organization, but not all add to it. Get in the habit of asking yourself if you are adding positively to the environment. Before making a statement or asking a question in a meeting, for instance, ask yourself, "Is this going to add and help or will it distract from the purpose? Am I offering solutions or problems?" When talking with others in the staff room, ask yourself, "Am I adding something positive here?"

The basic questions to ask yourself are, *What are my intentions?* and *What are the possible implications of this statement/action?* Checking in with yourself on a regular basis will help you maintain a consistently positive role in your company. We're not saying, however, that you need to be a yes man or yes woman. On the contrary, successful people often need to question the status quo or their colleagues' and supervisor's ideas. But if your intentions and methods are good, you'll know how to add in a productive, meaningful way.

Join a professional association

Professional associations are organizations that represent people who share a common background in a particular field or industry. These groups provide their members access to networking and social events, professional development activities, and career services. In addition, they may also conduct research about the field or industry; raise money for and organize charitable work that is somehow related to the field; work to attract people to the field by offering college chapters, mentoring, or scholarships; or lobby at the state or federal level for legislation that benefits their particular field. Joining a professional association will help you build connections and keep abreast of what's current in your field.

Get certified

Professional certification is available in nearly every professional field. In some fields – like nursing – certification at some level is mandatory. In others – like public relations – it is completely voluntary. Certification, especially if mandatory, is sometimes offered through government agencies, but is more often offered through professional associations or college programs.

Certification usually requires candidates to take a series of classes, seminars or lectures and pass one or more exams that test their knowledge of their profession. Certification may also require you to have a certain number of years of service in your profession, may mandate that you volunteer hours of service, and may require ongoing education and testing to maintain your certification.

Even if certification is not required, there are many good reasons to pursue certification in your field. Certification will help you stay up-to-date on the latest methods, research, and ideas in your industry; it will demonstrate to your employer and others that you take your profession seriously and are committed to growth and learning; it will help you develop new skill sets, knowledge, and talents; and it will inspire you to set both short-term and long-term goals for your career and professional development.

Continue your education

After graduation, it's understandable that you may need a short break from studying. But don't stay out of school for too long. Pursuing continuing education demonstrates to your employer that you are willing to learn and open to new opportunities – plus it provides skills and knowledge you need to do your job better and advance to more challenging roles. You don't necessarily have to pursue a PhD. One-day seminars, six-week classes, even an hour spent at a lecture will add to your expertise.

Choose your classes strategically so that you'll be able to apply what you learn in them to your current job or the one you'd like to have in the future.

Volunteer and lead

Everyone knows that volunteer work can have a meaningful, positive and lasting impact on communities, families, and individuals. It can also boost your career. Volunteering provides

- an opportunity to establish contacts, build relationships, and foster mentors.

- a platform to demonstrate your talents, skills, commitment and leadership. You may not be a manager at your job yet, but volunteering to manage projects and people at a charity can prove that you are up to the task.

- an important part of your growing resumé.

- the opportunity to learn new skills, gain new knowledge, and experiment with different interests and roles.

- a training ground for you to practice the skills you need to succeed in your career, giving you experience and self-confidence. Not sure you can deliver a high-impact project on a low-cost budget? Try it by volunteering for your favorite non-profit agency. When you succeed, your confidence will soar – giving you the courage you need to take on more challenging projects and roles at work.

- exposure to different perspectives and experiences, helping you to experience and appreciate diversity.

So, you want to volunteer. You know there are an endless number of organizations that need your time. But how do you find them? Consider the following:

- Contact your local government, United Way, colleges, or churches and synagogues and ask them to make recommendations.

- Visit your city, county, or state Web site. Many list local and regional volunteer opportunities.

- Search the Internet. There are a variety of volunteering Web sites that post volunteer opportunities or even match volunteers with organizations.

- Think about your interests and how you have been helped in the past. Were you a member of the Boys & Girls Club as a child? Do you remember being tutored by a volunteer at the library during middle school? Maybe you attended the summer arts festival of a local non-profit arts organization each year. All of these groups likely have volunteer opportunities – all you have to do is ask.

Once you've found a cause you're passionate about and a role that fits you, make sure you commit an appropriate amount of time to it. You want to bring energy and enthusiasm to your volunteer position without sacrificing your performance on the job.

Take care of yourself...

...or you're no help to anyone else. In order to do your work well you need to take care of yourself, too. So while we recommend volunteering for projects and committees, and certainly advise you to expect to dedicate many hours on and off the job working, it's also very important to take care of your personal needs. Sleep, for instance, is not an optional activity. Being your best at work means being your best, period. Alert. Focused. Personable. Even fun. So if you do choose to sign up for an additional project, do it well. Don't overextend yourself—you want to be professional, competent, and motivated rather than frazzled.

If you're lucky you're surrounded by supervisors and colleagues who share a desire to be way beyond average. In your company, the norm might be excellence and so "meeting the standard" means working at a very high level all the time. Such work environments can be incredibly supportive of both the individual's and the company's needs, inspiring every employee to work beyond his or her potential. Whatever your actual job circumstances, set high expectations for your own performance and you'll always be better off for having done so.

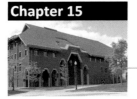

Chapter 15

INCREASE YOUR SALARY

The nip-and-tuck approach to finances—cutting coupons and eating rice and beans for every meal—only takes you so far. At some point, you just want to make more money. There are plenty of ways to increase your income, though not all of them are pleasant or legal. Some people take second jobs or start a side business or sign up to be medical test subjects at the local university or sell their roommate's stuff on eBay. A better, often-overlooked way to make more money is simply to ask your boss for a raise.

We're not suggesting you march into your boss's office after a week on the job and declare it's high time for a pay increase. However, after you've been at your job for a year or so, reflect on where you are and what you're doing for the company. If you deserve a raise, ask for it, and get it, that little conversation with your boss could translate into a salary increase of several thousand dollars or more. And it would probably be less painful than enduring another sleep deprivation study at the local university or your best friend's wrath when he discovers his prized Pez dispenser collection has been sold on Craigslist and shipped off to Paduka.

Sure, you could get turned down if you request a raise. So? "No" is the second-best answer you could get. Don't jump in quite yet, though. Requesting a raise is a process that involves a lot of thought and preparation before you even make the appointment to talk with your boss. This chapter covers salary negotiations as well as other ways you can prepare yourself now for moving ahead in your career.

Do you deserve a raise?

This is the guiding question. We all want more money and can imagine everything we'd do with a plumped-up paycheck, but when you ask for increased compensation you need to prove you really deserve it—first to yourself, then to your boss.

You deserve a raise if you…

- consistently exceed expectations
- have increased skills and education since you started the job
- perform significant duties beyond those outlined in your job description
- frequently work overtime in order to complete projects

When *you* are certain that you've performed at a level worthy of increased compensation, you'll be in a better position to sell your boss on the idea. The next step is to determine a fair salary for your work.

How much are you worth?

You have unique, inherent qualities that make you a special being interconnected with the other beings of this planet. Unfortunately, you don't get a paycheck for any of that. Your "worth," as we're using the word here, is the amount your organization's willing and able to spend to employ you. Determining factors include your skills, education, and performance on the job, as well as organization, industry, and regional standards.

Figuring out fair compensation for your work takes algebraic grace and some research. Dig around to find out what others in your field are making. Good resources for expected salary range:

How Much Should You Be Making?

There's no shortage of online salary calculators. Here are two that provide detailed information about comparable salaries— what other people with the same job title in the same region as you are making:
www.salary.com or www.bls.gov

- Online salary calculators

- Professional organizations

- Your university's alumni and career services offices

- Want ads and on-line postings

- Your organization's human resources department

- Coworkers (be careful with this one!)

Don't dig too much with your coworkers. Be sensitive to the atmosphere of the office and your particular relationships with colleagues. Some companies are very open, but in most environments salaries are confidential and it's not OK to talk about them.

How Much Should I Ask For?

You'll get a barrage of wildly different responses to this question from negotiating experts. The national average for raises in the last few years is fairly low: 2 - 3%. Your human resources department might be willing to divulge the company average; this would give you a sense of precedent and expectations.

Some experts recommend you ask for double what you really want. Others suggest a more conservative approach (asking for 7% when you know you'd be happy with 5%, for example).

If your job duties are drastically different from when you were first hired or if you discover in your research that you're significantly undervalued, you might swing a hefty pay increase.

If you do have information about coworkers' salaries, do not bring that up in your negotiations. You'll prove your individual merit better if you don't make comparisons to others.

Keep track of your accomplishments

Create a personal file filled with evidence of your accomplishments. Start it the first week on the job and add relevant pieces as you get them. What you're doing is compiling documentation that will prove (to yourself and your boss) that you are invaluable and working at a level worthy of higher compensation. Include all evidence of your productivity, salesmanship, teamwork, customer and coworker relationships, problem-solving skills, etc.

The goal? To document compelling evidence of the value you contribute to the organization. This file can also come in handy if you need to transition suddenly to another job.

Also, it's a good idea to update your resume every four months to stay sharp and focused on what you've already accomplished and what you want to achieve next. It doesn't need to be an official, perfectly-worded update. Handwritten notes will work just fine for this exercise.

Updating your resume regularly allows you to reflect on the good work you're doing, the skills you've mastered, and what you need to do next in order to stay fresh and marketable. It also gives you the confidence to make a move—whether it's asking for a promotion or interviewing at another company—when you feel like it.

Get noticed

When you do good work, you want to get noticed for it. Beyond all the warm, fuzzy feelings, the attention can also garner you a raise. Here's how to stand out:

Act confident. Believe in yourself and your abilities, and everyone else will believe in you, too. Avoid undermining yourself with comments such as " *This is probably a stupid idea, but…* " If you are modest to a fault, deflecting compliments and telling people you don't deserve your success (*"It really wasn't a big deal"* or *"Anyone could have done what I did"*), they'll believe you.

Participate in meetings. Meetings are a great opportunity to demonstrate your knowledge, skills, and creative thinking. Don't talk just to talk, but if you have something to say or to contribute, don't be shy. Make the most of your meetings by coming prepared, paying attention, and contributing when you can.

Expand your social circle at work. Meet and greet people from all departments, volunteer to serve on multi-department projects, get to know people from all areas – from the receptionists and the IT staff, to the accounting staff and upper management. The more people you know, the more chances you have to show your value. Plus, it just makes work more fun.

Share good news. You don't want to be arrogant, but you don't want to be invisible, either. Let others know when you do something notable. For example, copy supervisors and project teams on clients' complimentary letters and emails. After all, when a client or outside organization recognizes you, they're also recognizing your organization—so it's good news you should share.

Give credit where credit is due. Make sure you give compliments and kudos to coworkers. Do your part to create a positive, supportive environment.

Keep it positive. Even if the environment in your organization is cutthroat, try to keep your own contributions positive. Making yourself look good by making others look bad isn't only bad manners, it's a bad idea altogether. Earn your success through your own good effort, not through the mistakes or shortcomings of others.

Prepare for performance reviews

Performance reviews are used by organizations to evaluate the value of an employee, provide the employee important feedback on job performance, and to make decisions about raises and promotions. Performance reviews make many employees nervous and anxious, but don't sweat it. If you are a good employee, all you need is a little careful preparation to ace your performance review.

Performance reviews are different at every organization, but a few general kinds of reviews include:

Probationary review

Probationary reviews are what they sound like – they either precede or end a "probation" period. This probation period could be the period of time – usually 30 to 180 days – that some companies take to evaluate new hires before extending permanent, full-time employment. Or, it could be a period of time used to evaluate employees who have performed poorly in the past and are facing termination if improvements are not made. A probationary review can be performed at the start of a probation period to outline what is expected of the employee or at the end of the probation period to evaluate how well the employee has met those expectations.

Annual review

The annual review is the most common way to evaluate employee performance. The main focus of an annual review is to evaluate and highlight an employee's performance over the past year, develop strategies to improve the employee's performance, discuss short-term and long-term career goals, and determine if the employee is eligible for a salary increase of promotion. An annual review is also a time to let the employee know if he/she is not meeting company expectations.

Semi-annual review

Although not as common as the annual review, semi-annual reviews are used for the same purpose but are performed more often.

Self-evaluation review

Some organizations require employees to conduct a self-evaluation prior to a performance review. This ensures that the employee has considered and evaluated his/her performance and provides supervisors with a brief synopsis of his/her accomplishments, areas in which they need help or improvement, and goals for the coming year.

No matter what kind of performance review format your company uses, there are things you can do to prepare. To truly have a successful—and useful— performance review, you must put some time, thought, and effort into it. Make sure your performance review is a positive experience by doing the following:

Approach it as a positive experience. Performance reviews are useful to your company, but they also benefit you. The only way to learn, grow, and develop your career is to receive honest feedback and develop plans for ongoing improvement. It may be difficult to listen to criticism, but it will only serve to make you a better employee and a better person.

Develop a summary report of your accomplishments. This report is similar to a resumé, but outlines and highlights what you have achieved at your company in the time period that is being reviewed. Make sure you include all relevant information, but keep it as brief as possible – a page or less.

Compile documents that support the claims in your summary report. These documents can include letters and emails from clients, certificates of completion from continuing education programs, a portfolio of work, or budget statements that show costs cut and money saved.

Review any forms or checklists your supervisor has provided. Decide ahead of time how you will address each item or question. Identify any areas of concern and pay special attention to how you will formulate your answers to these areas.

Dress appropriately. Make sure you dress professionally on the day of your performance review.

Take notes during your review. Your notes may prove to be helpful as you create a plan to improve, and taking notes will demonstrate that you are taking the review seriously and are open to recommendations.

Avoid being defensive, making excuses, or arguing. Remember that part of your review is receiving criticism. No employee is perfect and everyone has room to improve. Try to view your supervisor's criticism as helpful and positive.

Toot your own horn. Your review is a time to identify areas of improvement, but it can also be a time to demonstrate to your supervisor all the areas in which you have excelled.

Use the feedback you receive. After the review, go over any documents your supervisor may have provided you, review what occurred during the meeting, and develop a strategy for how you will improve your performance in the areas that have been identified as needing work. Then, share your plan with your supervisor and be sure to document the steps you take to execute this plan. That way, you'll be prepared for your next performance review,

Timing

So you've been at the job for a year, consistently do superior work, and have taken on more responsibilities. Is it a good time to ask for a raise? The answer is "yes" if...

- The organization seems to be on an up-swing: good earnings (if it's a publicly traded organization this will be easy to find out), lots of new hires, and no shortage of resources.
- You have recently impressed others with your creativity, sales, performance, etc.
- Headhunters or representatives from another organization have been wooing you.

- You are due for your annual performance review. Note: it's easier to negotiate an increase in the amount offered at a performance review than to request a meeting and review mid-cycle.

- The region's job market is strong.

The answer is "maybe not" if…

- The company isn't doing well. Vacated desks, low earnings, rationed supplies, and negative news stories are all signs that it might not be the best time to ask for more money.

- You have recently made some mistakes or underperformed.

- The region's job market is weak.

Once you've determined that the company could probably afford to raise your pay (or that you're so good they can't afford *not* to), there's another bit of timing to consider: when to approach your boss. Schedule an appointment with him or her so that you'll have adequate time to present your case.

How to be persuasive

Most of us mastered the art of persuasion by practicing on our parents. Let's travel back in time. You're in high school and you want something from your parents. No, not unconditional love or wise counsel. You want to borrow the car because you have a date. And you believe you'll improve your chances of having a successful evening if you drive your parents' car rather than asking your date to hop on the back of your tricked-out, low-rider bicycle. What makes for a "successful" evening? Well, that depends on your perspective, which matters very much to you but is not necessarily something you want to share with your parents.

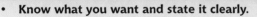

The Art of Persuasion   TIP

- **Know what you want and state it clearly.**
- **Understand your audience: How will the boss and the organization benefit by giving you a raise?**
- **Support your argument with evidence. Provide documentation of accomplishments.**
- **Anticipate opposition and be prepared to counter it.**
- **Always maintain a calm, reasonable tone.**

The best approach to getting what you want in this scenario is to focus on your audience's—in this case your parents'—wants or needs. If you say, "Mom, I want the car tonight because it's gonna make me look hot and I need to look hot because I'm really hoping to impress my date and…", well, let's just say that Mom is not likely to be convinced.

Similarly, your boss doesn't want to know how a higher salary will help you afford a new car or pay off bills or take a trip to Europe. He or she wants to know how it will benefit the organization. Your task is to prove your value to him or her in a calm and reasonable manner, using documentation from your personal file of accomplishments. Always, always remember that this is not personal; it's business. No tears, no temper.

Be willing to back up everything you say. If you declare an ultimatum—*If I don't get this raise, I'm walking*—you have to be able to follow through on it. If you have other equally or more attractive options than your current job, then you're in a better bargaining position and can take more risks. However, if you're fairly happy at the company or don't have other viable options, keep the stakes lower.

And the answer is...

...usually not simple. You might get a resounding "Yes!" to your proposed increase, but it's more common to hear "Yes, if..." or "Maybe later..." or "Not right now..." or "How about this...." (Again, very similar to dealing with parents.)

> **Consider This ...**
>
> ### The Line in the Sand
>
> Be willing to back up everything you say. If you declare an ultimatum—*If I don't get this raise, I'm walking*—you have to be able to follow through on it. If you have other equally or more attractive options than your current job, then you're in a better bargaining position and can take more risks. However, if you're fairly happy at the company or don't have other viable options, keep the stakes lower.

This is why you prepared so much going into the meeting. You know what you want, why you're worth a higher salary, and what's at stake for you. What you are about to learn is what they can offer you. Maintain an open mind. Maybe the company can't afford the full amount you requested right now, but your boss is willing to let you telecommute twice a week or can offer you some other flexible work arrangement.

Sometimes bosses will counter a raise request with a slight pay increase and a new title; that might be a good option if you're thinking of moving on in the near future as it will show well on your resume.

Work with your boss to devise a plan to develop your expertise and improve your credentials so that you can move up in the organization or at least move up on the salary schedule. The best employer-employee relationships are mutually beneficial.

Salary negotiations can get complicated and confusing, so always be ready to say, "This is a lot to think about. I'd like some time to go over these ideas on my own. Can we meet tomorrow to talk about this some more?"

Negotiating is part art, part science, and part poker. Do everything in your power to demonstrate excellence on the job, document it, and then calculate what that's worth to you and your employer. Successful negotiations depend on being able to read the company climate as well as your particular audience, your boss. Then, of course, there's the leap: Declaring what you want and waiting for the reaction. Sure, there's a risk. But if you keep your cool during the process, there's little to lose and a lot to gain.

MENTORS

Yoda. Dumbledore. Morpheus. In our quest to succeed, thrive, and do good in this world we all need a mentor. Someone to advise us, teach us to "use the force," and guide us to the next level.

No doubt you already have had a mentor or two: a trusted teacher or professor, an older student at your college, or a friend or relative who has served as a model and inspiration for you. As you begin your career, you'll want to find a mentor or mentors who can guide you on your professional journey.

Mentors defined

Mentoring is a one-to-one relationship based on encouragement, constructive criticism and feedback, and a mutual willingness to learn and share. Simply put, a mentor is an experienced and trusted advisor who is successful in his or her profession and has the ability and desire to teach and assist others.

Typically, the mentor is more experienced than the protégé. The protégé is usually someone trying to move up professionally and develop his or her career. The relationship benefits both participants. The protégé receives professional advice, guidance and nurturing. The mentor gets the opportunity to strengthen his or her leadership skills and the good feeling of knowing he or she is helping someone develop skills and experience.

Having a great mentor can be one of the most enriching experiences of your career. Why? A mentor can

- Help you set long-term career goals and short-term work objectives.

- Teach you about your organization, your profession, and how you can use your skills and talents to excel within them.

- Help you identify professional problems and create strategies and solutions for dealing with them.

- Give honest and useful feedback and criticism.

- Provide valuable contacts, invitations to industry events, and information and recommendations on networking in your profession.

Finding and working with a mentor

Many organizations offer mentoring programs. Some organizations even require new employees to participate in a mentoring program to help ease their entry into the corporate culture. Programs like these usually require you to fill out a questionnaire about yourself, your goals, and your working style. Then they match you with a more experienced employee in the organization.

If your company has a mentoring program, by all means participate. If your company does not have a mentoring program, you might also look into your alumni association, trade organizations in your industry, or professional groups in your area, as many of these kinds of groups also provide mentor programs. If, however, you don't have access to a formal mentoring program, you can still develop a great mentoring relationship. In fact, most mentoring relationships are informal.

Look for a mentor who

- Is established and respected at your organization and/or in your profession.
- Understands your organization's or industry's corporate culture.
- Has skills, experience, or talents that you admire and would like to develop.
- Is familiar with your position and the tasks/projects you work on.
- Is willing and able to devote the time and effort necessary to develop a good mentor relationship.
- Can relate to and get along with you, but is different enough from you to be able to stimulate your thinking and creativity and offer you something you can't learn on your own.

Now that you know what kind of person you are looking for, how do you find him or her and start the relationship?

Make a list of potential mentors. Develop a list of qualified candidates and rank them in order, beginning with the most qualified. Consider supervisors or managers at your company, work friends, acquaintances from professional organizations, past professors of subjects in your field, even previous employers.

Ask. Once you have decided who you would like as a mentor, ask that person if he or she has the time for and interest in a mentoring relationship. Explain what you hope to get out of the experience and what you hope your potential mentor might get out of the experience. Never pressure someone into being a mentor. Ultimately, you want someone who is enthusiastic and committed to the endeavor. If the person you ask is unable to serve as a mentor, ask if he or she can recommend someone else with similar experience.

Plan. Set up a schedule for meetings (you'll meet on the first Tuesday of every month, for example) and a timeline of goals you would like to accomplish with your mentor.

Once you have your mentor, make sure to make the most of your relationship:

Respect your mentor's time. Your mentor is making time for you in his or her busy schedule. Make sure you are always on time and prepared for your meetings.

Be prepared. When you meet, have a list of professional issues you would like to discuss, as well as questions and/or work you would like to share.

Be professional. You and your mentor may become good friends over the course of your relationship, but you should do your best to keep the mentoring time professional. During mentoring meetings, avoid discussing personal matters.

Stay open-minded. You have asked your mentor to provide you guidance, advice and feedback. Make sure you are open to his or her comments and avoid being defensive.

Provide feedback. Let your mentor know if their guidance or advice has helped you master a skill, finish a project successfully, or earn a promotion.

Express gratitude. After every meeting send a note or an email thanking your mentor for his or her time. If you meet over lunch or coffee, pick up the tab. If your mentor's help results in a great promotion, raise or other recognition, you may even consider a small gift. And, if your mentor works at your organization, consider letting his or her boss know just how much you have been helped by copying the boss on a letter or email of thanks.

Make the relationship a priority. Don't let your mentoring relationship stagnate because you feel you don't have time or energy. If you find that scheduling becomes an issue, discuss alternate arrangements with your mentor. And remember that this relationship is important to your career and deserves all the time and effort you can contribute to it.

It's easy to hyperfocus on the day-to-day tasks that make up a job. But when we put our heads down, put our noses to the grindstone, etc. it's easy to lose sight of bigger, more meaningful goals. Having a strong relationship with a mentor takes time—both yours and your mentor's—but it's a great way for both parties to get perspective and develop professionally.

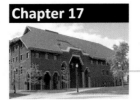

Chapter 17

NETWORKING

You've heard the saying "It's all about who you know." However, a better statement is "It's all about who knows you." This has never been truer than at this time in your life. Developing a group of contacts and mentors—in other words, networking—is one of the most important things you can do in your early career.

Networking keeps you tapped in to the ideas, trends, and information that are relevant to your profession, makes you more visible, and helps you connect with others. However, networking doesn't necessarily come naturally. Like any other skill, it must be developed to make the most of your opportunities. Here's how.

What is networking?

Quite simply, networking is the act of meeting people with whom you can develop mutually beneficial relationships and exchange information, advice, contacts or support. A few examples of networking are:

Example 1

You attend an industry cocktail party and begin a conversation with an executive at Company X. You know for a fact that your company would love to do business with Company X. During the course of your conversation, you mention an article that the executive expresses interest in reading. At the end of the night you and the executive exchange business cards. On Monday, you email the executive a link to the article that you discussed. A few weeks later, the executive emails you to let you know that his company is looking for the services of a company just like yours to help on a specific project. You let your manager know the information you have received. Your company submits a proposal and wins a big contract—and you get big points with your manager.

Example 2

You attend the monthly meeting of your industry trade organization and meet several young professionals in your industry. After giving one of these young professionals a tip on a great restaurant to take clients to in her area, she invites you to have lunch next week with her and several of her colleagues from a company with similar interests as your. You begin to have lunch on a regular basis with this group. A few months later, a job opening that is a perfect match for your skills and talents opens up at their company. Because of your inside information and a few good recommendations from your lunch group, you land a new job—and a $7,000 pay raise!

Example 3

While attending an industry educational seminar, you make small talk with other attendees during the morning break. In the course of one conversation, one attendee mentions that his daughter is trying to get into the very same college that you attended. You offer to have lunch with his daughter to coach her on what she needs to know about the college—and he offers to introduce you to his best friend, who just happens to be a top-level executive at a company that you would like to sell your product or service to.

You will notice one thing that all three of these stories have in common: both parties gained something out of the exchange. Networking is all about creating and acting on opportunities; ideally, your role in your network will be to help others as much as it will be to connect with others who can help you.

Why network?

Networking isn't always easy, but it's important. Networking in the early stages of your career can help you land jobs, secure promotions, develop your understanding of your profession, and gain important insight into what it takes to succeed in your field. As your career progresses, networking will likely remain an important activity, as it provides professional insight into clients, sales leads, potential business opportunities, and career advancement opportunities.

If you are a friendly, open individual who likes to meet people and help people out if you can, you've already met most of the criteria of a networking pro. If you tend to be more introverted, you can build confidence through practice. It might feel forced at first, but after a while networking will begin to come naturally.

How to network

So how do you build your network? First, determine who can help you. Start with what you know, including:

Your college. Many schools have alumni associations that are great places to network, or even offer lists of alumni who are willing to speak with other alumni about professional opportunities.

Family and family friends. Your relatives or their friends and associates might have connections in your field.

Advisors and supervisors. Look to former professors, teachers, coaches, and employers.

Members of groups you belong to. You probably already know many people from clubs, churches, teams, and associations. Some of them might become good professional contacts, too.

Your friends. Your friends and their families might have connections in your industry or field.

Next, research additional opportunities for networking, including:

Professional groups. There are probably trade organizations, industry associations, and professional clubs that you can join.

Educational opportunities. Seminars, classes, professional development workshops, educational speeches, forums, and talks are all great venues to learn about your field and make connections.

Networking organizations. There are organizations that meet on a regular basis with the sole purpose of establishing a place for people to network.

Volunteer work. If you volunteer, you'll probably meet like-minded people who may also have connections in your field—or the field you want to get into.

Social occasions. Gallery openings, grand opening parties, holiday open houses—these types of events are great opportunities for networking.

Finally, develop a sound strategy for networking:

Have a great elevator speech. An elevator speech is a synopsis of who you are and what you want people to know about you that can be delivered in the time that it takes to ride an elevator a few floors. Figure out what is important about you and boil it down to a minute or less.

Establish and maintain a professional online presence. Join the listserves and other online groups relevant to your profession, join networking websites such as LinkedIn, and use Facebook as a professional tool. Chapter 18 goes into depth on these topics.

Be prepared. Always bring business cards and even copies of your resume wherever you go.

Be engaging. This includes being friendly, confident, open, and interesting. Make sure you are up to date on the latest industry trends and current events so you have something to talk about.

Be interested. Project a genuine curiosity and interest in other people and what they have to say. People are drawn to people who like them. The person who listens well is going to end up with more contacts and interesting connections than the person who monopolizes conversations.

Drop names. When appropriate, let people know if you have friends or colleagues in common.

Build relationships. People are more likely to stick their necks out for you if they feel they have a relationship with you. Don't ask people to go out of their way early on. Instead, take some time to build the relationship and see what develops. If you ask for a job right away, the person might say no – and be turned off. If you stay in contact over the course of a few months through email, lunches and meetings, you might be the person who naturally comes to mind when a job opens up.

Be helpful. If you go into networking only focused on what's in it for you, you'll come up empty handed. Networking means that both parties help each other. In other words, you have something to offer as well. Spend some time thinking about what you have to offer. It could be information, contacts, skills, or support.

Keep track. Develop a system of tracking your networking contacts. Keep your business cards in a binder, update your Rolodex on a regular basis, and add contacts to your email address book.

Be respectful. Ask permission before passing on anybody's contact information, don't call excessively, and avoid coming across as if you are always looking for a favor.

Show gratitude. If someone does something nice for you, thank them! Email is fine some of the time, but don't underestimate the power of a written note. Depending on how extensive the help was, you may even owe someone a lunch or a gift.

Keep at it. Networking isn't something that stops when you get to a certain point. Just because you landed the job, the client or the contract, doesn't mean that you want cut your networking ties. Maintain your network. Email, write, and see your contacts on a regular basis. You never know what kind of great things might pop up – or what kinds of things you can do for other people.

Ultimately, networking is all about relationships. And the best relationships are mutually enriching. Consider your role in your network: there will be times when you'll need to call on others for assistance, advice, and favors and other times when you'll be the one assisting, advising, and doing what you can to help somebody else out.

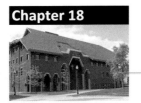

Chapter 18

YOUR CAREER
AND THE INTERNET

You've heard the idea that everyone is connected to everyone else by just six degrees of separation? Well, make that just two degrees of separation, thanks to social media such as Facebook, LinkedIn, and Twitter. Because of this, your online presence—and the relationships you build through social networking—is vital to building your career.

The majority of people still find jobs and get hired through personal connections. Social media is your route to making more personal connections—and to making them more, well, personal. As we mentioned last chapter, the old saw "it's not what you know, it's who you know" has morphed into "it's not just who you know, it's who knows you." Which leads us to a critical question: What do people know about you? If they know you're skilled, trustworthy, and hardworking, they will be happy to help you connect with others. Having a strong network not only gets you the job—it also gives you the opportunity to exchange ideas and knowledge with other professionals.

Now is the time to create a professional online presence and start building valuable connections. In this chapter we'll discuss the major social media sites and how you can use them to grow professionally.

Grandpa, what's Facebook?

For as long as there's been social media, there have been people predicting its death. As of the printing of this book, however, it's still very much around. Facebook, as of this moment, has 750 million active users. Because of those numbers, we'll assume you're already familiar with Facebook. LinkedIn, a professional networking site you might not be using yet, has over 120 million users. On LinkedIn, users post their profiles, including job experience and education, resumes, and interests. LinkedIn individual members use the site to make professional connections and exchange ideas. Companies use LinkedIn to find new hires. If Facebook is casual Friday—or very, very casual Saturday night—LinkedIn is business-attire Monday. Facebook lends itself to informal, personal exchanges; LinkedIn is your best reflection of your professional self. Another popular means of staying connected is Twitter, which people use to post short updates or to track their friends, favorite celebrities, and organizations. There are countless other social media outlets, which ebb and flow in importance and numbers of users.

Establishing and maintaining an online presence

When you're ready to use social media for professional purposes, you've got to take a look at your current online presence. Google yourself and see what others can easily find out about you. If you have blog posts, pictures, or other things online that could potentially sabotage your chances of finding and keeping a job—or that could inhibit your ability to connec t with others in your profession—consider deleting them, if possible. Employers, potential employers, colleagues, and others *will* search for you online and you need to be comfortable with what they might find.

After you've taken stock of your current online profile, take steps to build a professional online presence:

1. **A good first career move is to join the organizations relevant to your profession—or the profession you'd like to have.** Sign up for relevant Facebook groups, Listservs, or other email groups and check them regularly. Make sure you consider all groups that might benefit you professionally: National, regional, and local professional organizations; alumni groups; and specialty interests that relate to your current or future professional goals.

2. **Create a profile on a professional networking site, such as LinkedIn.** Upload your resume and request recommendations from professors or previous employers. Approach online requests for favors such as recommendations just as you would in the real world: Show that you value the person's time and assistance, be specific about your request, and follow up with a thank you email or note.

3. **Make Facebook a positive or neutral force in your professional life.** Decide who you want to view your Facebook profile. Clean up your profile, posts, and page if possible. Check your privacy settings. Facebook is notorious for changing privacy settings regularly and not providing very clear directions about dealing with those changes. Luckily, if you Google "Facebook" and "privacy settings" you'll find plenty of tips on how to tighten your privacy settings. Privacy online, however, is always best considered an oxymoron.

Consider This ... **Who are you online?**

Your online personality may be a factor in whether or not you're hired, fired, or promoted. Consider these two examples: One applicant for a marketing assistant job had all the qualifications, but made a bad first impression before she even set foot in the interview room. Her interviewer Googled her and discovered, among other things, a blog post filled with profanity. She did not get the job. Unfair? Possibly. But it's certainly not an isolated case. Another example is a chef who ranted about his employer on his blog, and made sarcastic comments online that damaged the restaurant's reputation. He was fired immediately. Everything you post online—and even those things posted about you—can potentially help or sabotage your career.

Making connections

Both Facebook and LinkedIn are excellent for networking and provide a window that up until a few years ago wasn't available. Remember that the rules of engaging professionally online are the same as they are in the real world: Introduce yourself and demonstrate your respect for the person's time by keeping your messages short and by not flooding the person with requests or information. Be gracious, too. For example, some people limit their LinkedIn connections to a small circle of very well known, highly trusted individuals, and will not accept your invitation to link up until they get to know you better. Also, consider your situation carefully before friending a boss or colleague on Facebook. Do you want that extra level of connection with them? What are potential drawbacks and benefits of being Facebook friends with people at your particular workplace?

Finding a job

Social media can be an essential means not just to finding a job, but to finding the right job. From a simple Facebook status update or tweet: "Anyone know of any accounting positions open in Austin?" to a more targeted LinkedIn search for a position in a particular department in the organization of your dreams, you have a powerful job search tool literally at your fingertips.

If you find yourself needing a job, first get the word out. Post what you're looking for and follow up any tips you get from people with an update or thank you. If you find yourself wanting another job—but not ready to tell your colleagues or supervisor that you want to move on—you might have to be more targeted about getting the word out. You don't want your boss to find out and have, at best, an awkward conversation and, at worst, a burned bridge.

Next, search for companies and organizations that interest you and determine if you have any personal connections to someone working there. For example, you might see that one of your contacts on LinkedIn is connected with someone who works in the field you want to get into. You might contact that person—a so-called "second-degree contact," akin to a "friend of a friend"—and request information or let him or her know of your interest. Note: Common practice is to limit such messages to second-degree contacts. In other words, reach out to a contact of a contact, but not a contact's contact's contact. Even if you don't have connections to an organization, you can get a lot of information about it and potential job openings by searching its website and following it on Twitter and Facebook.

If you build a strong online presence you might find that you won't have to do a job search: people will seek you out and make you an offer. They might hear about you through tweets, retweets, a LinkedIn connection, or something you've published online. Or, your blog or Facebook posts might draw just the right kind of attention.

Remember to update and thank people who help you out in the process of finding a job. They'll appreciate the follow up.

Social networking and the workplace

You might have a job that requires you to be plugged into Facebook and Twitter all day, but if it's not part of the job description you should probably avoid social media activity while you're on the clock. We know one person who was fired after he called in sick the same day he posted on Facebook pictures of himself enjoying the sun at the beach. Another acquaintance was such an active Facebook status updater that it was hard to imagine she was able to get any work done in between the updates. (A colleague, tired of having his email requests to her ignored, once sent a Facebook notice from his cubicle next door: "When you're done with Facebook, would you mind going over the document I sent you yesterday?")

Social networking is certainly not dead. It's a powerful force in the social and professional lives of countless millions of people. It can backfire—being tagged in those pictures from Cabo, for instance—but follow common sense and social networking can be an incredibly enriching and positive force in your professional life.

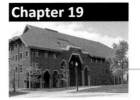

Chapter 19

UNEMPLOYMENT

Recession, unemployment figures, consumer confidence index—most of us are more familiar with these terms than we'd like to be. Ah, for life before we ever heard "toxic asset" or "bail out." Oh, for the days when "double dip" referred to ice cream cones, not an economic trend. While unemployment has always been a potential side effect of being in the workforce, we have to be especially savvy about it now that the unemployment rate in the U.S. hovers around 9%. This chapter covers how to avoid being laid off or fired as well as methods to recover from unemployment.

Signs you might lose your job

People who have been laid off or fired often say it came out of the blue. One day everything was normal, the next day they were frozen out of their organization's intranet. Often, however, there are some clues that the company's not doing well or that your position isn't secure. Here's what to look for:

Industry trends. How are your competitors doing? Are other companies in your industry experiencing layoffs, bankruptcies, or other difficulties? If so, it may be a bad sign for your company as well.

Organization trends. What is your company's financial status? For example, has the company lost a big client or contract lately?

Cost cutting. Is there a lot of talk of cutting costs and budget cuts? Is the company in a hiring freeze? Has there already been a round of lay-offs somewhere in the company? Are a lot of normal expenses being cut back – travel, expense accounts, support staff, supplies?

Bad news. Is your company at the center of negative news articles or a scandal?

Skimping and late payments. Have you noticed that bills from suppliers and service providers are being paid late? Has your paycheck been late or bounced?

People jumping ship. Have managers and other higher ups been resigning? If so, this could be a sign that they know something negative about the company that you don't know.

No new hires. When people quit or are fired, does your company assign their duties to other existing employees rather than hire new employees to replace them?

Change in management. Has your company changed hands, been bought out, or completely replaced its management?

These kinds of clues relate to organization or industry issues that might affect you. In other words, they are signs that you might be laid off, one of the cost cutting measures your organization takes. The following clues are more personal.

Here are signs you may be fired:

Conflict with supervisor. Are you in constant conflict with your manager or supervisor? Is he or she documenting his or her interactions with you more regularly and in more detail—creating a "file" on you?

Poor performance. Have you received a poor performance review, failed to meet performance goals, or been put on "probation" or a performance improvement plan?

Frozen out. Are you being left out of "the loop"? In other words, are you being left out of information, meetings, projects and events that you normally would have been a part of?

Major mess up. Have you made a major mistake or misstep that you suspect could cost you your job? Everyone makes mistakes, but sometimes a mistake is so big that it cannot be overcome, even if it wasn't completely your fault.

Bad attitude. Have you been told that you have a bad attitude?

Passed over. Have you been passed over for a raise or a promotion that you expected?

Left out. Are some of your job functions being reassigned to others? Have others at your same level in your company been sent to professional training or given perks that you have not?

Distancing. Does it seem like people are avoiding you? Are coworkers harder to get on the phone? Does your supervisor avoid looking you in the eye? Has your office been moved to a more remote location? Those may be signs that people are distancing themselves from you because they have heard that you are about to be fired.

The indispensable employee

So you've caught wind that big lay-offs are heading your way. Now what? Make yourself an indispensable employee—one that your company can't live without. It won't necessarily ensure that you won't be laid off eventually, but you might be able to buy some time to line up your next opportunity.

Ultimately, you want to do more in your profession than just keep from getting canned. The following traits and habits foster job satisfaction and success, while also making you indispensable—or, less dispensable—and more likely to be promoted or get a raise.

Develop skills. The more you know the better off you are. Even being the only one who knows how to use a program or software, un-jam the copier, back up the computer system, or create a spreadsheet can add up in a manager's mind to someone whose skills are essential. Learn as much as you can and use your knowledge to help your company.

Become an expert. Concentrate on what you're good at and develop an expertise on that subject that's unrivaled by anyone else at your organization.

See the big picture. Understanding how your job functions and how your department's work fit into organization's overall mission, or big picture, can help you be more efficient and effective in your work. And, because you understand how the company works, you are adaptable to other job functions, making you a valuable company asset.

Volunteer. Volunteer to help wherever you can and take on any project you think you can do well. Knowing that you're a go-to person who is willing to take on all projects—big and small—can make you essential and hard to part with. Just be sure not to overextend yourself; taking on so much that you can't do your work well will not impress your supervisors.

Think creatively. Someone who brings new and exciting ideas to the organization is always essential.

Communicate well. Good communication is essential in just about every field. If you can speak well, write well, and generally represent the company professionally, you will be seen as an asset.

Be positive and collaborative. Difficult people are usually the first to go in a reduction of force. Having a good attitude, being friendly, and being willing to work on a team all make you easy and fun to work with – an asset that will may help you keep your job.

Document your success. Keep a folder of your successes so you can prove just how valuable you are to the company if you should need to. Keep a record of clients you have landed, money you have saved the company, projects successfully completed, your ideas implemented, and other job achievements. Don't be a braggart, but make sure those in charge know about your successes by copying them on key memos and emails and keeping them informed of the status of your work.

Be flexible. In times of crisis, organizations look for employees who can roll with the punches. They want employees who can take on new job functions, put in extra hours, or adapt to new and changing corporate culture and expectations fit the bill.

Cut costs. Lay-offs usually mean that your company is in crisis – and in cost-cutting mode. If you can prove that you and your work save the company money, rather than cost it, your job will be more protected from cuts. Does your job function increase production, land new paying clients, help reduce wasted time, effort or resources? Figure out how your job adds to the bottom line. And if it doesn't, figure out a way to make sure that it does.

Be a self-starter. Managers operating in a lay-off environment are stressed. Anything you can do to reduce this stress will be seen as a plus. Employees who need constant supervision, feedback, and direction are usually the first to go because managers figure that they put so much effort into maintaining the employee's work that they might as well do it themselves. The more independently you can work the better.

Understand that relationships count. Being friends with the boss and putting in face time at the office doesn't guarantee that your job will be spared, but it doesn't hurt either. Creating meaningful work relationships makes your job more fulfilling and more secure.

What to do if you're fired or laid off

If you are fired or laid off, there are things you can do to minimize the damage of your unemployment and to start the search for a new job. Even if being laid off or fired is the furthest thing from your mind right now as you embark on your new career, you should plan for the worst to avoid being caught completely off guard. Here are some tips for successful unemployment:

Participate in the exit interview. There are probably so many things you'd rather do with your time, like eat shaved glass or listen to talk radio at full volume. However, the exit interview can be a valuable experience for you and your former employer. During an exit interview, you can voice your opinions about your employment—and you might learn how to perform better in your next position. Just be sure to take the high road, no matter how tempting the alternative is. Tempered honesty is fine; tactless complaining is not. You may hate your boss, but telling the HR rep during your exit interview that he is a complete jerk won't do anyone any good. Letting them know that you could have used more constructive criticism and realistic deadlines might help them guide your former manager to a better management style.

Always keep your resume current. Even if you think that being fired or laid off is a remote possibility, you should keep your resume up to date. Make it a monthly habit to update your resume, develop your list of references, and add to your portfolio of work. You never know when that unexpected job offer may come your way.

Leave on good terms. Don't do something that you might regret once your emotions have calmed – you never know who you might encounter later in your career.

Ask for a recommendation letter. Even if you have been fired, you probably know someone at your company who would be willing to serve as a reference and/or write a recommendation letter for you. Ask for it now, while you and your performance are still fresh in this person's mind and while you are still in daily contact.

Ask about a severance package. Some companies offer employees generous severance packages, especially if they have been laid off. If you are eligible, spend it wisely. It may be all you have to get you through to your next job.

File for unemployment. Your employer has been paying unemployment insurance on your behalf during your employment, and you are now eligible for the benefits. Don't let your pride stop you from taking this important step. You don't know how long you will be unemployed, and your unemployment checks may be a big help financially. Contact your state unemployment office to find out what you are entitled to and how to collect.

Contact your creditors – If you have student loans, personal loans, a mortgage, car loans, or credit card debt, you should contact your creditors to let them know that you have lost your job and may have difficulty making payments for a short amount of time. Many creditors have programs in place to help customers through unemployment, and allow reduced payments, deferment of payments, or at the very least may agree to waive late fees or finance charges or hold off on reporting late payments to the credit bureaus. Make the call before they start calling you.

Check out COBRA – The Consolidated Omnibus Budget Reconciliation Act (COBRA) gives employees who have lost their jobs the right to choose to continue their employer's group health insurance for a limited period of time, at the employee's expense. In other words, if you lose your job, you don't have to lose your health insurance. Even though you will have to pay the premium cost yourself, you can continue to subscribe to the same health plan that you had while you were employed, usually for up to 18 months. Although the several hundred dollars you might have to come up with each month may seem hefty, you are better off continuing your healthcare coverage than not. If you get ill or injured and do not have health insurance, your healthcare costs can be in the thousands or even tens of thousands – a debt that can take years to overcome. By law, your employer should provide you all the information you need to continue your healthcare insurance coverage through COBRA.

Evaluate your financial situation. This is the time to make a budget and stick to it! Assess how much you have in savings and budget that money to last you for as long as you can.

Consider unemployment a job. Make job hunting your new vocation. Set aside a place in your home as a "home office," set your alarm each morning and "go to work." Devote as much time to job hunting as you would be devoting to a job, if you had one. That means eight hours a day, five days a week – and some overtime if necessary. This is also the time to practice your interviewing skills, capitalize on your network of contacts, and brush up your resume and cover letter writing skills.

Stay healthy. Losing a job is stressful, whatever the circumstances. It can also be embarrassing, expensive, time consuming, and frustrating. Keep stress at bay by keeping it in perspective. Stay positive by viewing your unemployment as a time to reevaluate your career goals, revitalize your commitment and passion for your profession, and reignite your career.

Prepare your script. You may feel like keeping your unemployment a secret, but it's not a good idea. Being honest and letting people know that you are unemployed and looking for a new job is one way to get the word out that you are available for hire. You'd be surprised at how many people are willing to tip you off on job leads, put a good word in for you, or make a phone call on your behalf when they find out you are unemployed. Prepare a "script" of what you will say to people regarding your job loss so that you are less nervous revealing your unemployment. You don't have to give every gritty detail of how or why you were fired or laid off; in fact, it's important to avoid sounding bitter or deflated. Just let people know that you and your employer have parted ways and that you are in the market for a new career challenge.

Track your expenses. Costs associated with finding a new job can be deducted on your taxes. Check with your accountant about the details, but make sure to save all receipts of any job-hunting expenses as you go.

Unemployment is a stressful and challenging time for most of us. If you find yourself without a job remember that you are not alone. Do whatever you can to stay busy and productive; your determination will pay off in the long run.